The Finding 40 Project is a journey. Over nearly two years, 10 countries and thousands of miles, these women graciously gave their time and opened up on the most personal of levels to share their experiences at 40 and the events that have shaped their lives.

Each chapter stands alone, with a respondent's answers framing a peek into her life and the challenges and opportunities that shape her days.

There is no author commentary about the women or their responses; it's not my job to tell readers how to feel about each woman's journey to 40.

I could not have completed this project without the incredible support, love and help from countless friends and family all over the world. A special thank you to PCI Global for their partnership and assistance locating women to interview, my parents, for not cringing too much when I announced my next interview destination, my sister for her unending support and love for my efforts, the HWIMs for their incredible cheerleading and assistance with my 40th birthday celebration and photo showing and last, but not least, Jefe, for accompanying me on this crazy journey and well, just being Jefe.

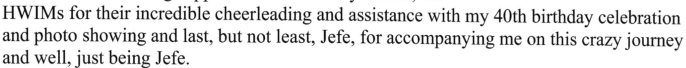

I hope you enjoy this compilation as much as I enjoyed meeting and getting to know these amazing women.

Amy

New York, New York USA

"In this crazy world of access and excess I try to keep my kids grounded"

You could say life is a little hectic for Amy. She's juggling a full-time, highly public career as a reporter on ABC's "Good Morning America," raising two daughters and three step sons and somewhere in between trying to find ways to squeeze in time with her husband, Hollywood actor Andrew Shue. She's called her family "one step away from a modern-day Brady Bunch" but seems to be relishing the constant flurry of activity.

We talk with Amy via Skype after she's already had a long day; 4 a.m. wakeup, 5 a.m. arrival at work, on air until 9 a.m. then meetings, details and planning for the next day. In between she's taken her daughters to school and managed to grab a quick bite with Andrew. She has just a short window to chat before she's off again to pick her daughters up and later take them to ballet class. Despite a schedule that would make most people's heads spin, she's friendly and relaxed, comfortably hunkered down on the floor at home for our interview.

One of the first things I ask her about is her public life; with both she and her husband being photographed, I wonder what the advantages and disadvantages are about being a celebrity. She laughs, slips in a joke about being a 'd-list celebrity' and adds "we're not that famous, but sometimes we get recognized and photographed. Most of the time, if we are riding the subway or sitting in a restaurant, people leave us alone and most everyone is fairly well-intentioned. Our kids though are pretty amazed that people know who we are. One particular day, when I took my daughters to the Good Morning America studio, there were paparazzi outside and they shouted to them 'hey, Amy's girls, look over here' and they got photographed. I worry about that, that they might think that's a measure of self worth -- that someone wants to take your photograph," she says.

She finds she has to be more cautious of what she does in public now, a concept unknown to many people. "I might be sitting at a restaurant and I realize someone is sitting next to us, tweeting about what we are doing and saying. I stop for a minute and begin editing myself."

Although the public lifestyle presents challenges, it also opens up unique opportunities for both Amy and her children. "I have gotten incredible access to 'pinch me' moments through my career, such as the funeral of Ronald Reagan, the inauguration of Barack Obama, having my kids meet their favorite teen idols -- My daughter Ava got her photo taken on Miley Cyrus' lap! They see celebrities like The Jonas Brothers and Justin Beiber quite often and really don't have an understanding of the hype surrounding superstars. To them, it's just another person that mom works with; they don't realize how unusual their life is. In many ways that's a good thing, because it allows them to see celebrities not on a pedestal, but just regular people, which they are."

Despite being surrounded by celebrity, Amy tries to give her kids that same upbringing she experienced. "I have Midwestern, Catholic and German values -- I believe in rules and expect a lot from my kids. I don't reward for good behavior; they are *supposed* to be good. Some of my friends and work colleagues joke that I'm a 'mean mommy' and I'm actually totally OK with that. I know I am giving my daughters the foundation they need to grow up to be strong, financially independent women."

At ages 6 and 9, her two daughters have their own bank accounts. "They earn stars for extraordinarily good behavior or extra help around the house. When they get 7 stars, they get $7. I don't just give them $7 in cash, however; I transfer the money into their bank accounts and they each have their own debit card to learn about budgeting, saving and spending."

Circling back to her near Brady Bunch status, I ask Amy if there are plans to add another child into the mix. "We're in discussion about that," she says and laughs. "I've gone back and forth about it; we have five kids now, ages 6 to 16 in the house. I'm not a star-struck young mom; I know how hard it is. I'm not sure I'm ready to go back to diapers and late-night feedings. Andrew had a great comment about this: You never regret having a child, you only regret not trying, and I agree with him. We think we would try for a year and if it doesn't happen, that's it. Maybe that will be my 40th birthday present to myself!"

Amy never thought she would be at this point with such a robust family. "I came from a big family; my mom was one of nine and my dad one of six. Growing up, I never thought I would even get married, let alone have kids. Now, I've been married twice and have five kids -- go figure!"

She and Andrew connected in 2009 as both of them were going through a divorce. "One of my friends and co-workers was going to a charity event with Andrew. While planning for the event, Andrew had lamented that he was lonely, with his three boys and wanted to meet someone nice. He asked my colleague if she knew anyone. 'As a matter of fact, I do!' was her reply. She convinced me to attend the charity event and told me about Andrew. I was unsure; I wasn't really looking to meet anyone at that time. We met and five months later we were engaged and 10 months later we were married. Who knew!" she laughs.

Despite both of their hectic schedules they commit to making time for one another. Sometimes it means Andrew joins Amy on assignment, but there's no guarantee their entire trip won't change or get cut short. "Our vacations are often my shoots but inevitably something comes up. Earlier this year we were in Turks and Caicos and I got called back to Detroit to cover a major story and interview a serial killer. You just never know."

While she has traveled the world for work and met amazing people, she finds the more intimate interactions the ones that impact her the most. "Sure, when you go to a city to cover the Olympics they roll out the red carpet for the press and it's fun. The stories that stay with me the longest are ones like a nightly report where I met with people waiting for hours in the freezing cold of Appalachia for space heaters. Early in my career, I witnessed an execution. The prisoner had a bad reaction to the lethal injection and it was a very violent death. Everyone in the room had taken a vow of silence and it was surreal to sit there and process it all; it took the breath away of the priest standing next to me.

I've covered the aftermath of a hurricane where you see a person who has lost absolutely everything. Those experiences show the resilience of the human spirit and I am amazed at what people can live through and flourish," she says. "I often say I get to see the best, the worst and the weirdest the world has to offer."

- *Biggest Accomplishment*: My daughters.

- *Biggest Regret*:   Getting married so young and focusing too much on my job...I didn't have the fun and freedom I should have had.

- *Biggest Surprise at 40*: My divorce.

- *What Would You Do With an Extra $100?*   Spend it on a good meal. *With an Extra $1,000?*   On designer shoes. *An Extra $10,000?* On a trip to Italy.

Anabel

Avignon, France

"I never really thought about what life would be like at 40 when I was younger"

The late afternoon light is slowly painting everything pinkish-gold in the ancient fortified city of Avignon in southern France. Sitting on a terrace just steps from a centuries-old church, we talk with Anabel about her life in France as a photographer and single mother.

"I never really thought thought about what life would be like at 40 when I was younger...when I was 25 I looked ahead and was happy I was starting out in my career – I had just started to really make money and was on my own. It was good, I could travel, explore places and see things," she says. One of her first assignments as a press agent photographer was to go to China for a piece on one of the country's wine regions near the Great Wall. "I went for two months – one month to work, one month to travel through southern China on my own...I loved it."

Over the course of her career, Anabel has worked for three different press agencies. Her longest stint was 10 years with Gamma Press and then working for a different agency specializing in people and politics. She has shot numerous regional events such as the large Festival de Avignon and the Contemporary Art Fair in Paris. "I studied cinema and photography in university and liked it; my first work was with a little club in the

university shooting photos for events." After that I started taking pictures – my first work was with a little club in the school shooting photos, after that I was an assistant on a small town for the Opera – after that I started with the Avignon Festival." She's

moved on to even larger shoots, including positions as an official photographer on major motion picture shoots and the Cannes Film Festival.

Seven years ago Anabel's life changed dramatically with the arrival of her daughter, June. She and the father never married and are not together now. She speaks of a difficult relationship between them and that he "does not make things easy for her" in their everyday life. Anabel currently has custody of her daughter every other weekend, with June spending most of her time at her father's.

You can tell speaking with her the situation is not to her liking. "He is not nice," she comments. Working as a photographer she is able to have some flexibility in her schedule but if she is traveling she will not see her daughter for some time. A true photographer's daughter, June takes Anabel's camera and snaps lots of photos of us as we talk.

"I grew up in the small village of Séguret until I was 16 and then went to Lyon for two years and one year to Nîmes to study photography," she says. "Like many people, I came to Avignon because it was a bigger city with more opportunities. I met June's father here and then we lived for one year in Spain in Andalusia. We were only together for one year after June was born although we were together for 9 years total but never married – I didn't want to get married." Anabel returned to Avignon to pursue more photography opportunities and to be closer to her family.

One of the more unique work assignments came through a local private detective. A local woman suspected her husband of infidelity and hired the Avignon-based sleuth. Anabel was commissioned to travel to a town outside of Hong Kong to try and catch him in some impropriety where he was working at an electric station. "The husband didn't want to divorce and the detective knew I had been in China before." She went under the ruse of documenting and photographing the work project and each night would photograph the group, including the husband. The last night, she couldn't find the group in its regular space and later located the dinner party up on the roof, ringing in Chinese New Year. She got the photo she needed.

Looking ahead, she hopes to have more time with her daughter and do more traveling. She went with her mother to Sri Lanka at 17 years old and since has traveled to Italy, China, Indonesia, Hong Kong and Singapore. She didn't really contemplate life at 40 when she was 30, and doesn't think about 50. When I ask her about life 10 years in the future, she has a playful smirk and twinkle in her eye..."I really don't think about it. One of my best friends is 51 and she says it's OK, so that's good!"

- *Biggest Accomplishment*: She stops and thinks a moment, then says "I am most proud of my daughter, my friends, my work and my mother." Her mother still lives in small village near Avignon and Anabel sees her once a month at least. She and Anabel's father are divorced but he still lives nearby as well and is a regular part of her life.

- *Biggest Regret*: I wish I had more control over my life. I would like to travel more. I've never been to Africa, Thailand, Japan nor the United States and would want to go there.

- *Biggest Surprise at 40*: Watching my daughter grow as she has really learned to read and write in the last year a lot. My life completely changed with that and she goes to school in the small village nearby.

- *What Would you Change if you Could?* I would like to have another child, but I don't know if it's possible at this point. I would like to have a larger family and work more on films. Last year I worked on a film in Paris called "The Art of Seduction" – I would like more assignments like that.

- *What Would You Do With an Extra $100?* I would buy a new camera and travel. *With an Extra $1,000?* She laughs – the concept doesn't seem possible. She says "I don't know – I would try to go to see the moon. My neighbor was an astronaut." *An Extra $10,000?* If I won that kind of money, maybe with Bingo, I would give it away to charity to create a school, a real building with running water, etc.

Casey

Fort Collins, Colorado, USA
"Wearing Pantyhose and Sitting at a Desk Was Not for Me"

She breezes into the offices at New Belgium Brewing Company fresh off her motorcycle, blue eyes sparkling ready to tackle the discussion of 40 head on. She stops and looks down doubtfully at the camera. "Is this a photo interview too?" she asks. "Geez, I would have worn a little makeup or dried my hair; it's all matted down from my helmet! "

Unaffected, Casey swipes on some tinted lip balm and jumps right into the interview.

Although she graduated with a bachelor's degree in business with an emphasis in finance from Colorado State University, she knew that wasn't the career path for her. "I went into to college really just trying to grow my own personal knowledge and I had the most credits accumulated toward the finance concentration, so that's where I ended up."

No Wall Street career for this one, however.

Nearly 10 years ago she started at New Belgium Brewing Company as a "Sales Ranger" (representative), serving most of the western half of Colorado, servicing accounts all over the region. She was on the road five days a week but loved it.

Within a few years she moved on to be an event manager, where she basically "went to all these awesome mountain towns and threw parties and everyone was always happy to see me." These events required a lot of driving however and physical labor with keg transport and setup/teardown. Even though it was tough, Casey loved the drives, surrounded by gorgeous scenery sometimes for up to three hours at a time.

A miscarriage in 2006 and the eventual birth of her first daughter in 2007 heralded a major lifestyle shift. Lugging kegs wasn't feasible with a swollen belly and long hours on the road weren't conducive to care and feeding of a newborn. As is the case with many members of the New Belgium family, her title shifted and she moved into a new position as an administrative assistant to the company's "eventers" (event directors) and eventually as the executive assistant to the director of sales. Casey and her boyfriend

welcomed their second child, another daughter in March 2010, "at the ripe old age of 39" (she adds with a sly smile and giggle).

She and her boyfriend have been together and committed since 2004, wear rings on their left hands, but don't have plans to marry. "I would avoid it if I could," Casey adds, "I guess if at some point our kids would like us to get married...If they felt weird about it or something, then I guess I'd do it." The morning of the interview came after a rather sleepless, kids-up-most-of-the-night, leading Casey to wonder out loud if she "would be crazy to think about more kids when I see how tired I am at times like this."

Financially, Casey and her boyfriend are running a balancing act as a one-income household. "We are a bit unusual; my boyfriend stays home with our kids while I work full time." They became a one-income household when their oldest daughter was just three months old; his full-time position as a French teacher was going to part-time with no benefits.

After running the numbers for child care, factoring in the boyfriend's 70-minute round-trip commute to work each day, they decided it just wasn't financially worth it for him to continue in a part-time teaching role. "My income supports the entire household so it can be a struggle to pay the bills each month; however, we are so lucky to have one parent stay home full time with our kids. We have a lovely home, are able to provide for the girls, but it's always a bit of a dance each month. I'd love him to get a full time job in the future to help ease the financial strain."

When asked about her impending date with the big 4-0, Casey says: "I absolutely think it's awesome. I loved turning 30, I felt like I was so much wiser and more mature...now though, I look back at 30 and realize I was such a young punk. 40 for me is about becoming a mother and really watching my children grow." Many of Casey's close friends are also turning 40 in the next year and originally a small group had planned to go to Europe together to celebrate the milestone. "Kids, jobs and life started getting in the way, and Europe turned into a trip to Las Vegas, then a weekend in Los Angeles...Eventually we ended up having a three-day slumber party at one of our houses. It was fantastic. We did have a fancy night on the town one night, but the best was the next night when we all sat around the house, drinking wine and having deep discussions about being 40 and what it meant. It was empowering to be around a group of women that each had 40 years of knowledge to share."

She was hired at New Belgium just a month before turning 30 and had no real thoughts beyond the next month of work. "For someone who never planned on having kids, if you told me at 40 I'd be looking ahead through the next decade and could see myself at 50 dealing with my daughters' pre-teen hormone drama, I would never have believed it!"

- *Biggest Accomplishment*: Although we struggle sometimes month to month, I am proud of what I have been able to accomplish financially on my own – proud that I put myself through college, found a great job and purchased a home on my own! I now am on my third house that I have bought without anyone's help.

- *Biggest Regret*: I don't have any regrets. I do get disappointed about physical things out of my control related to aging.

- *Biggest Surprise at 40*: Wow, I really have to exercise and watch what I eat. I never had to really work at it, it's a big surprise. That's recent, as of my second daughter.

- *What Would you Change if you Could?* I would change the financial piece – it's really the only main struggle we have. If we had just a little bit more so I didn't have to worry every month. I don't want anything fancy, I just don't want to have to worry each month.

What Would You Do With an Extra $100? Today I would buy groceries. *With an Extra $1,000?* Put toward my credit card balance. **An Extra $10,000?** Pay off the credit card completely, the rest to my kids' college fund.

Catherine

Rome, Georgia, USA
"You bloom where you are planted."

After finishing college and going to photography school, Catherine lived near New York and in London, worked in advertising and traveled for years as a photographer's assistant. She was confident she would not be heading back home to the historic town of Rome, Georgia. This city of just under 40,000 is about an hour or so northwest of Atlanta, and is home to classic Antebellum estates and a quaint downtown with a Broad Street dotted with brick-facade business, some dating back almost 200 years. Like its sister across the Pond, this Rome boasts seven hills, though these roll with vibrant green fields filled with cows and country cottages.

However, her path brought her back to Rome and Catherine's surprised at the outcome: She's happier than she ever thought she could be back home in the south. "When I went off to college to study photography, I was confident I was destined for a high-profile career and that I would do something great, though I didn't know what that was. "I am simpler than I thought...It really doesn't take a lot to make me happy, and I am surprised by how normal my life is."

"When I first finished college, I worked in Connecticut just outside of New York for a year and then after art school I moved to London to find work as a photographer's assistant, determined to have a life far, far away from Rome. It was a lot of anxiety and worry about finding the right job and the right husband...it was such a waste of time to be so terrified. I wish I had traveled more, risked more and not been so afraid of being alone. I wish I had not underestimated my potential then."

Sitting with Catherine, her truly genuine southern charm and ease seems so perfectly natural it's hard to imagine her anywhere else but here. We photographed her on the campus of Berry College, a breathtaking setting with grand quarried stone buildings around gorgeous parks, lakes and fields. She takes a look around the campus and blends right in to the country setting. "You bloom where you are planted," she comments.

Many people associate the south with a level of hospitality not seen elsewhere. But is it true? Catherine believes so. "I think there is a feeling from people who don't live in the south that the hospitality is not truly genuine. People in the north might be inclined to think there is a 'fakeness' to it, a lack of sincerity … I know I saw that first hand when I lived in the north. I feel like it's real though...Our pace is like how we talk...a little slower and a little more dragged out. Here, when there is a need, whether financial or personal, the southerners have a way of comforting not just with words, but with food, visits and overwhelming sweetness. That's what comes to mind when I think of southern hospitality."

Now, she and her husband work hard to maintain that

ideal and to live the way her parents and grandparents lived. "I love our almost old-fashioned sort of life and wouldn't trade the blessing of being a wife and a mom with anything. We play outside, have family movie nights and dinners at the table together five nights a week." Their two children (Elizabeth, 10 and Toby, 4) enjoy a type of family stability many around the world have no concept of. "We spend most of our time together as a family and we love it. As a team, we have consciously decided make sacrifices to live below our financial means so we can save for our family's future."

Standing at the milestone of 40, Catherine has a different perspective from when she was 10 years away.

"I remember thinking 40 was way over the hill - now that I am there I feel nowhere even close to a hill.

When I was in my twenties, status was what I had hoped I would have at 40...A big house, successful career and an active social life. When my children came along everything changed and it wasn't just about me anymore."

Catherine can see how quickly her children are growing up and whenever she hears older women advise, "Enjoy this time, it will be over before you know it," she knows to heed their warning and savor all the fun little quirks that come from these years. "I have figured out that contentment is an attitude, a choice and happiness has nothing to do with status like I thought it would. "I aim to live for the blessings I have now rather than setting my eye on what's next like I used to."

- *Biggest Accomplishment*: Our family life.

- *Biggest Regret*: When I was younger, I wish I had more confidence in myself and my ability to succeed with a happy life.

- *Biggest Surprise at 40*: From where I was right out of college, I am surprised by how "normal" my life is.

- *What Would you Change if you Could?* I would have worn sun protection and taken better care of my skin. I would have exercised more when my body was younger.

- *What Would You Do With an Extra $100?* Cover the grocery bill for the person behind me in line. *With an Extra $1,000?* I would love to treat my friends to a girls' weekend. *An Extra $10,000?* Take a trip with my family and pay what is left over toward our mortgage.

Cristina

Torino, Italy

"I ended up quitting my job, selling everything and buying a plane ticket to Italy...I came home."

Born in Torino, Cristina's life has crisscrossed the globe. Her parents were living in Abidjan, Ivory Coast in Africa when her mother was pregnant with her, and chose to come back to Torino (their home town) to deliver their daughter. It would be 32 more years before this nomadic soul called this northern Italy city home again.

After she was born Cristina's mother brought her back to the Ivory Coast, where her father was working as an engineer in the oil industry. Her twin sisters three years younger were also born there. The family remained in Africa for several more years, eventually transferring to Montreal, Canada for a completely different way of life. "I was born speaking French so transitioning to Montreal was not too difficult," she says. A few years later, the family relocated again, this time to English-speaking Toronto. Cristina took English lessons alongside her mother and now considers herself a native English

speaker, although now she is also fluent in Italian as well. Both her parents were multilingual, speaking Italian, French, English and some German.

Switching gears again, the family headed to the United States – to the deep south in Houston, Texas. Because Cristina's father was still working in the oil industry, the family remained in the south, relocating again to the tiny town of Bartlesville, Oklahoma, all before Cristina hit age 14. Cristina found some permanence when the family moved to New Orleans and she spent her high school years in The Big Easy and began her university studies there as well. "I've always been very curious, looking around for new adventures and opportunities – I guess it's in my blood."

While in university she met and married a US Navy Seal, which took her life in a whole new direction – to sunny San Diego, California. "We were married for 12 years but it was really difficult. He was always deployed, away on missions somewhere in the world and ready to leave within 24 hours. We never even took a vacation together. That's a tough way to make a marriage work." Eventually, it didn't work and the pair split up. "Thank God for my friends and career during that time. They kept me sane and became my second family in many ways." Cristina eventually decided to venture off on her own to New York, continuing the career she began in New Orleans and continued in San Diego with Saks Fifth Avenue.

She was moving to New York to be a buyer for Saks; a dream job. Her timing ended up being anything but a dream. The move to New York was scheduled for the week of September 11, 2001. "I remember packing, trying to get everything ready for the move and watching everything on television...I couldn't believe it. Even my employer called and told me they would understand if I didn't want to make the move and changed my mind about the job all together."

Undaunted, Cristina was determined to move on with her new life. "I was on the very first flight into New York from California. It was surreal – I was one of like six people on that flight. Moving to New York in that time period was bizarre. The world was not the same." One upside she discovered though was that normally the stereotypical New Yorker is not willing to lend a hand; everyone was now all too eager to lend a helping hand. "The very first day of work there was a bomb scare on the subway, we were evacuated and I had to get off far from my scheduled stop. I was lost, confused and some very nice people helped me find where I needed to go!"

For three years Cristina lived in New York, moving on from Saks and joining an individual fashion brand, working in product development and market research. "Honestly those three years were not the easiest, both personally and professionally. The world in general was a bit tough. On a positive side, I also had some amazing experiences and had the chance to meet some of the most interesting people including many famous designers, which was both exciting and inspiring at the same time. Nonetheless, I decided it was time for another change though. I ended up quitting my job, selling everything and buying a one-way ticket to Italy."
She returned to Torino, the city of her birth.

Although she had neither a fixed plan nor place to live, she wasn't worried. "I love to travel, it's in my blood, and I figured if I ever wanted to go live in another country with a new language and culture, it was now or never." After living with an aunt the first month, she located a small loft-style apartment just off a lovely piazza.

"I thought it would be really interesting and I was ready to discover where I was from. I have always had some family here and I had started to come frequently for vacation – first once a year, then twice, then I thought, 'I'm being drawn here more and more so maybe it's time to discover my roots and where my family is from.' I thought I would just see what happens, and if it didn't work out, I could always go back." So far it seems to be working for Cristina; eight years in and she is still happy in Torino (although, you never know where she could end up next!)

"I am very proud of my traveling, having been to 27 countries and 326 cities, my accomplishments and who I am today – I've done it all on my own. I am in a happy phase – I think, '40 is OK, it's good and not as harsh as I thought. I definitely feel comfortable in my skin. I have learned and finally acquired a real confidence in myself ' – I feel like I've changed my philosophy on life. When I used to think about 40 and what I wanted to be doing, I was influenced by all these standards and norms people want you to live up to. You need to be doing and have X, Y and Z to be successful and happy. I don't feel that way any more and feel like I am changing the way I see things – that everyone should be happy with what they have done and their own personal and unique journey, even if it's not exactly what they had imagined for themselves, and I certainly am. There's a time and place for everything and I believe things happen for a reason. It's never too late to be the person you might have been."

Making it on her own is an obvious point of pride for Cristina. "I've basically lost it all several times and had to fight my way back, but I'm still here." After first holding product development and market research positions with various European brands, she now works exclusively as an independent contractor, consulting with different companies around Europe and often helping to create collections with designers. "For two years I worked for a London based company and I was commuting so often between London and Torino that I had an apartment in each location; towards the end they actually wanted to relocate me permanently to London. The commuting was getting to be too much, but I wasn't ready yet to make another move after just two years. I wanted to just stay here in Italy full time and really give this place a chance."

Her traveling nature means she continues to take on innovative projects around the world. "Besides my regular consulting business I also have a made-to-measure men's suit business that takes me to Switzerland and India. I've also worked as a model and actress, doing print work, commercials and film for many years and now am even jumping into theater!" Cristina guesses it's her love of performing that has drawn her into these ventures.

From a young age, Cristina loved to dance, specifically ballet. She attended some of the best schools, including Tulsa City Ballet, the New Orleans Center for the Creative Arts and the North Carolina School of the Arts and studied classical ballet, modern, jazz, character and flamenco with various famous teachers and attended summer stage sessions as well. While Cristina was living in New Orleans and performing with the Delta Festival Ballet, one of her instructors from Oklahoma came to visit and told her she was moving to Milan where she would be teaching at the world-famous Teatro alla Scala. The instructor thought she would be an ideal fit for the young apprentice program and wanted Cristina to move with her. It was every young ballerina's dream. Her parents refused. "I had been training for this my whole life and I was crushed; even after high school they wouldn't help me get into a dance program. There was a lot of family drama going on at that time and I feel like my dreams were put aside for their needs. I left home and started working to support myself and fell into the fashion industry at 19, working full-time at Saks in New Orleans and attending university at night and on my days off.

"Now, I still try to be very active in the arts and support artists wherever I can. What I'm realizing now is that this time is for me. I want to pursue my own interests and my new dreams and not follow someone else's; or go by what society thinks I should or should not have done at this point. I guess with age comes a little wisdom. Even though I haven't been close to my family, I know you can make your own family with friends wherever you go. I'm lucky to have created that wherever I've landed I and I know I have friends I can count on in all corners of the globe who will always be there for me."

- *Biggest Accomplishment*: Myself. Becoming the person that I am today – It's emotional for me I guess because I have done it all on my own. My life hasn't been the easiest because of several factors – relationships, family, and disappointments – but I have always gotten through the challenges. I educated myself and I raised myself. I've done it all on my own – and I am proud of that – it could have gone a very different route. Who knows where I might have ended up? I am proud of the person I have become because of my strong values; I try to live my life with honesty and loyalty and expect the same from others. I've always moved forward and never looked back. You can't change the past but you can shape you future. I've had to make some brave decisions at times but I believe, you just have to have faith that it will all work out in the end, because it has to. In working through the fear of the unknown I've acquired a new kind self-confidence. I've done the best I can with myself and in stopping to think about my life for this project, I think I've done pretty well despite the hardships and am finally giving myself more credit than I usually have in the past. I now choose to be happy!

- *Biggest Regret*: I don't really regret anything I've done in my life but I regret not having had the chance to try to fulfill my dream of becoming a professional ballerina...but everything happens for a reason.

- *Biggest Surprise at 40*: I thought that maybe at this age I would be more financially stable. But again, there have been circumstances because of the economy where I have lost everything and started over a couple of times, and I've been able to do it. I've had the strength, willpower and talent to start over. I feel like a cat with 9 lives; I've already lived so many! At one point, I also thought I would have a family of my own at this point, but I don't and that's OK.

⋏ **What would you Change if you could?** I wish I could have had more support from my family at a young age when I most needed it. If I did have a child, I would never forget their dreams. I feel like my dreams got pushed aside for other priorities – my father was always away traveling for his work and his projects, then my parents divorced, my father left and my mother was battling her own issues, and feel I was forgotten in the midst. By leaving me very much on my own, on the other hand, my parents instilled in me some very hard-core working values which I don't regret since they have helped me get through the toughest of times. Moreover, I am fortunate that they took my sisters and me around the world and exposed us to different places, people and cultures, never discriminating and being open to everything the world has to offer. There is always something to learn somewhere or from someone new and this is where my love of travel comes from.

⋏ **What Would You Do With an Extra $100?** I would put it toward a lavish pair of shoes or a wild accessory! (She says with a bright laugh) **With an Extra $1,000?** Use it towards and airline ticket or trip to somewhere I have never been before, maybe Japan…or Thailand…or Australia. **An Extra $10,000?** Put it aside or invest it...maybe toward a property or another investment and make it grow.

Dionne

San Diego, California USA

"I've had a lot of money and I've not had a lot of money; now, homeless, I'm at the most content point in my life. That's weird, isn't it?"

It seems practically impossible not to like Dionne. From the moment we meet, she is upbeat, friendly and personable, despite the fact that we are meeting in a residential shelter. Dionne's been living at St. Vincent de Paul Village for the last three months and she's been homeless since 2010. St.

Vincent de Paul Village is a partner agency of Father Joe's Villages, Southern California's largest residential homeless services provider.

Her journey to homelessness began in 2009, when she lost her job as a taxi dispatcher and clerical assistant. She couldn't find a new job and decided to put her energy into a new career, completing her certification as a Medical Billing Specialist but it didn't help. "I still couldn't find a job and no one wanted to hire a specialist without any experience. I couldn't catch a break." After a while she lost her apartment and was living on the streets and with friends. "It was not a good time," she adds. The final straw was losing her car, which severely limited her ability to apply for jobs or work anywhere outside public transit lines.

Losing her car wasn't completely without benefits though. "I'm actually in the best shape of my life," she says with a chuckle. "Since I had to walk everywhere, it forced me to do more movement than I have ever done. The weight just fell off; I didn't really change my diet but it just kept coming off and I've lost 100 pounds already. People really didn't start to notice until I had lost almost 70 pounds, but it has been great for my health." A new dedication to a healthier lifestyle seems high on Dionne's list. "Even when I get a new job, I want to stay active, keep moving. Right now I am applying for jobs at the shipyards, because I will get to move every day."

Dionne became aware of the homeless services at St. Vincent de Paul Village when she stayed at the temporary Winter Shelter in downtown San Diego. "I'm a very independent person and don't like to have to rely on someone, but I couldn't live on the streets any more." After the seasonal Winter Shelter closed, Dionne 's health was deteriorating and she ended up in the hospital, diagnosed with Rheumatoid Arthritis. "When I got out of the hospital, I was in bad shape and could barely walk. St. Vincent's knew me from the Winter Shelter and were able to get me a bed at the residential community right away."

Though her accommodations are very modest, they are clean, comfortable and safe. "I share a cubicle space with another woman with two bunk beds; I'm the bottom bunk. I get my own 5-drawer dresser and one drawer under my bed. We've got 50 women on the floor and we all share a community bathroom with seven toilets and eight showers...It's incredibly clean!" Part of that cleanliness comes from the fact that each resident is assigned a regular chore connected to the maintenance of the facility; Dionne's daily duty is staffing the elevators for residents and guests.

The day we meet is an especially hot one in San Diego. Dionne tells me the air conditioning in her building has not been working for the last two days but she doesn't mind. "I am truly blessed. I've had a lot of money and I've not had a lot of money. I'm at the most content point in my life. That's weird, isn't it?"

I probe a little deeper into this comment asking why she is most content now, being homeless. "I know myself better than I ever have, I know what is best at for me at 40 and how to take care of myself."

Ten years ago Dionne wasn't taking very good care of herself. "When I was 30, I couldn't see ahead to 40. I was using a lot of drugs. I couldn't see past that day; I was null and void," she says. Ironically, Dionne gained weight on crystal meth, her drug of choice, one that often causes users to become quite thin. Her overall survival chances were in jeopardy. "My family gave me a choice: Go to rehab or lose my children. I went to rehab and got clean. I was 32."

Her children, now grown, live in Northern California in the Bay Area. A 22 year old daughter attends the Art Institute in San Francisco and her 18 year old son just graduated from high school. "He's working two jobs right now so he can have his own apartment for him and his girlfriend," she adds obviously proud. The two children are from two different fathers and Dionne is not in a relationship with either. Never married, she has essentially been a single mom the whole time. "The child support checks did come and that was helpful, but otherwise I'm on my own."

Dionne's own father died in 2003 and her mother now lives in Northern California as well. "Both of them gave endlessly to me and my brother and we pissed away the opportunities. My brother is a bit of the 'golden child' and is living in San Francisco with my mother; I am trying to take care of my grandmother here. When he became homeless they couldn't fathom that thought so they took him in. It sucks."

Watching her children continue to grow and succeed is an immense source of pride for Dionne. "I can't wait to be a grandmother. I wanted to get myself together for my kids and I did."

Her healthier lifestyle is a big part of this next chapter in her life. "I was fat even from a young age, and it really kept me from doing things. I was an outdoor person but didn't know it...the weight kept me indoors. The more I lose, the more I am outside." She talks about hiking a popular local mountain peak, anxious to get out and conquer it. "I thought I hated being outside, but I really hated it because I was fat. I guess I never knew that part of myself!"

Next up is a new job and getting out of the shelter. "You are allowed to stay here for four months with no strings. After that, they help you to try and get disability/SSI, or a job. I'm on the career track. I qualified for disability but that's not my style. I'm going back to work." Dionne doesn't want to be confined to a life of $900/month, which is what she would receive on disability. "I see everyone all around me, fighting to get on and keep disability because you don't have to work. I want something better; I want a job and my independence." Asked about life 10 years down the road, Dionne says "I haven't looked ahead yet. If I applied for disability at 50 I would be going nowhere. When I look ahead with the thought of a job, I am excited. If I do what I need to by then, 50 will be great."

- ⅄ *Biggest Accomplishment*: My children. Despite my issues, they have gone on to do what they are supposed to do.

- ⅄ *Biggest Regret*: When my children were young I didn't spend enough time with them physically.

- ⅄ *Biggest Surprise at 40*: My weight loss. It just happened, I didn't plan it. I was overwhelmed. My doctor wanted me to get bariatric surgery but I resisted. I don't need it now, I can keep going on my own!

⅄ *What would you Change if you could?*   I would love to have a home, an apartment. I want a good job to get stable.

⅄ *What Would You Do With an Extra $100?*   A bicycle! I've wanted a bike. *With an Extra $1,000?* I would give it away. I would help my children, they both could use it more than me. My son does not need to take care of me, I wouldn't interfere in his life. He's 18, he needs to have his own life. I would never make my son take care of me. *An Extra $10,000?*   It's funny, I've had that before, but I was heavy into drugs. Right now I couldn't fathom it. I would get an apartment, pre pay some rent and get settled.

Emma

Dubai, United Arab Emirates
"Do you want to hear an interesting story...?"

It seems perfectly fitting to interview Emma next to a ski slope in the middle of the desert. We meet at a coffee shop next to "Ski Dubai," inside the Mall of the Emirates. Surrounded by an ocean of sand, this glittering city of gold rises almost impossibly, with the world's tallest building, the Burj Kalifa, brushing the sky. The ski slope seems completely at home in a land of excess.

We begin speaking about her life in Dubai as a wife and working mom of two boys, running a successful events management company. Emma came to Dubai as a young girl with her parents more than 30 years ago from the United Kingdom, and now calls both places home. As a young woman, she split her time between the two, attending boarding school in the UK and visiting with her parents at their home in Dubai.

After graduating from school, she attempted to find work in the UK, but found it difficult without an advanced degree and decided to return to Dubai for opportunity. After talking a bit about her various career choices before beginning her own firm in 2004, she leans in close across the table, and in an almost conspiratorial tone, she asks, "do you want to hear a good story about living in Dubai?" Of course the answer is yes. It seems the mirage of Dubai is not all Louis Vuitton and Lamborghini after all.

"My husband spent eight and a half months in jail here," she begins. On November 2, 2010, her husband was arrested as he was taking one of their sons to school, taken into custody by Dubai plain-clothed policemen. Her husband David had been tagged with a "Security Check" for bouncing checks. In the United Arab Emirates, bouncing a check is the same as stealing and carries a heavy legal penalty.

The problem was, the only reason her husband had bounced a check at all was because of the Dubai government itself. He and his business partner ran a construction company, working on several large projects for the Dubai government during the region's boom time. Huge skyscrapers and retail complexes were going up at a dizzying pace during the late 1990s and early 2000s; money and scope were no object.

In 2009, Dubai's bubble burst. As much of the world's economy began to enter recession and see the effects of a crumbling housing market and credit crunch, the money in Dubai began to dry up. Projects were left half-finished and developers went bankrupt. David and his partner thought they were going to be OK since their primary projects were with the Dubai government, not private builders.

However, that ended up not being the case at all. The government skipped out on payment for the work David's firm had done, leaving them millions of dollars short. They attempted to pay their suppliers to honor contracts, but the funds weren't there and checks bounced. They were considered criminals, even though the basis for their "criminal" actions came from the Dubai government itself.

Like thousands of others in the same position, David and his business partner were arrested and charged; he was taken into custody immediately. "I was 39 and had two young kids to support, I didn't know how I would get though it," Emma says. "We didn't have his income and I had to support the family...We had to move since we couldn't afford our current house."

Emma worked to keep her sons' lives normal. "For a while, I didn't even tell them what was going on. Thankfully, when my husband was arrested it was a plain-clothed officer in an unmarked car so my son wasn't aware what happened," she adds. Emma says both she and her husband never actually thought he would go to jail. "We thought it would be some questioning, maybe a fine, and that was it...
he got a three year sentence."

Emma credits her mother as being an amazing help and rock during this time. "We tried to make sure that our family continued on normally and I also was helping with repatriating staff from my husband's company back to their home countries during this time. I thank God I had her with me," she says.

Emma and other "angels" (as she calls them) worked tirelessly to try and get her husband and business partner out of jail. One of their options was to try and get assistance from their local business partner. Like most businesses in Dubai, all foreign business owners cannot truly "own" their business. David and his partner owned 49 percent of their company; a local partner owned 51 percent. This practice is common in many countries trying to minimize foreign ownership of local operations.

They needed signatures from the local partner to help release funds to get David out of jail. The local partner was happy to help...for $100,000. Emma was floored. "We were basically blackmailed," she said. "They told us they would get us the signatures we needed and help with the case, but only if we paid them the money first. I was shocked."

For the first time, Emma's view of Dubai had been tainted. "When I came here, it was really almost like a little fishing village, full of opportunities and I loved living here; my parents loved living here. Now, our perspective was forever changed," she said. It didn't matter that the whole reason her husband and his partner were in jail was because the government failed to pay on their contracts. "I really saw that the legal system was in the dark ages here," Emma adds.

Finally, after eight and half months, David was released. His business partner is still hoping for release. "Although it was a very dark time, that entire situation brought us back to our core partnership in many ways," she says. "I try not to let things get the best of me and I have to look at what came out of that situation. Our family is amazingly strong and I was able to take care of my boys on my own; that was very empowering to know I could do that."

Now that the ordeal is over and David is back home and working again on construction contracts, comes the million dollar question: Why stay? "I don't want to do anything rash or hasty," Emma says. "I don't have any roots anywhere else at this point in my life; my parents are here. I was able to support us with my business which was amazing for me and I'd like to see that business grow." Still, Emma plans to make a change in the future.

When both her boys are in full-time boarding school in the UK she plans to return there permanently. "I have amazing people around me and it's hard to decide, but I don't want my children to grow up and live here – I want to go back to the UK. Even though I have lived here most of my life and have a business here, in many ways we are treated no differently than someone who just got off the plane. The justice system has a lot to answer for."

- *Biggest Accomplishment*: My biggest accomplishment that I feel I have achieved in my life is to raise two boys that are so very kind to others, that are loving, are polite and incredibly funny and entertaining to be around. People are always commenting on how well they've been raised and I feel incredibly proud when I hear that.

- *Biggest Regret*: I have no regrets. Maybe the only thing that I have found to be disappointing is not having that fairy tale marriage I have always wished for. Whilst trying to remain a realist that maybe there is no such thing, there will always be a part of me that wished I was cherished more, that I was loved more and for all what I have achieved in my life, respected more by my partner.

- *Biggest Surprise at 40*: It has taken me 40 years to realize just how resilient I have become. I have tenacity beyond what I ever thought imaginable and when looking back on situations that I have been faced with, when at the time you can't see light at the end of the tunnel, I have been surprised to find out that I have handled it with decorum and wisdom when perhaps 10 years or maybe even as little as five years earlier I may have been more hot headed and rash that may have resulted in very different and not such a positive outcome.

- *What Would you Change if you Could?* I don't think I would change very much in my life to be honest. I have no regrets and I try to embrace my life with vigor, sense of adventure and excitement. My glass is always half full and I always strive to get the most out of my life.

What Would You Do With an Extra $100? Spend it on my children. *With an Extra $1,000?* Spend it on my children and myself. *An Extra $10,000?* A portion of this would be spent on my children and myself and I am sure some of this would be used to improve something in my business. I would most definitely use $1,000 to have an afternoon/evening with my best girlfriends drinking ourselves silly as a celebration of finding the money!!

Erasma

Chinchero and Cusco, Peru
Language barriers don't stop a kind heart…

Erasma speaks no English. My Spanish is so-so at best. A translator is not readily availble. However, with a warm smile and traditional kiss on the cheek, Erasma agrees to have her picture taken and attempt our interview.

Cusco is a cultural hub for Peru, home to countless beautiful handcrafted artisan products and textiles. Erasma lives in the village of Chinchero, about 45 minutes outside Cusco, where she works in traditional handicrafts and loves to dress in customary Peruvian colorful clothing. During the week, however, she spends her days hustling with the rest of the staff at the hotel where she works near Cusco's historical Plaza de Armas.

We chose the picturesque plaza as a photo setting, attempting to

capture a bit of Erasma's exuberant energy that mimics this bustling town. All day long I watch her at work, jumping between cleaning tasks, literally running up and down multiple flights of stairs with laundry, cleaning products and deliveries for guests. Cusco's at 11,300 feet; I'm out of breath just watching her.

After we speak for a bit and take photos, I ask if I can give her a list of questions I've prepared in Spanish and if she would mind writing her responses; I can translate them later. With a large smile, she agrees and says proudly, "I can write."

One of Erasma's most interesting set of responses came when she was asked about what she would do with an extra $100, $1,000 or $10,000. With none of these windfalls would she spend money on something fun or personal. Instead, she would choose to use the funds to expanding her weaving business. Textiles are a huge business in Peru and handicraft stalls cram the cobblestone side streets heading in all directions from the Plaza de Armas.

With $100 she would buy supplies for the artesian co-op she currently participates in (perhaps yarns, dyes or equipment for a loom). When the number jumps to $1,000, she would like to create her own store or business for selling her wares. At $10,000 she is thinking large, and would form a small company with employees to create a variety of crafts. One of her greatest regrets is not being able to get a loan, primarily for being a female. Her pride in her weaving skill glows brightly; her face shines when she explains to me the work she does in her village of Chinchero.

Erasma's most important moment in her life so far was a trip to Guyacail, Ecuador with her artesian craft group. They were sponsored to bring a showcase of their skill and finished work and it further reinforced her love for work in the craft trade.

Although Erasma loves her work as a weaver and craftsperson, you can tell she has a desire for more. When asked about where she thought she would be at age 40, her response is interestingly "living in another country."
Looking ahead to 50, it appears she still dreams about a life outside her native Peru, hoping for other opportunities.

She's interested in potentially exporting some of her work to other countries clamoring for her initicritely woven tapestries, cloths, scarves and wraps.

Similar to some of our other South American interviewees, 40 doesn't seem to be much of a milestone. 50 appears to be the mark to hit. Maybe 40 really just is a number? It certainly is to Erasma.

Gloria

Quito, Ecuador

"When I was 30, I was still looking for me….Now I feel like I have found myself."

Gloria movies quickly and easily between tasks in her role as receptionist at a hotel in bustling Quito, Ecuador. Although she has multiple projects running at any one time, she effortlessly greets each guest with a smile and answers countless questions about restaurants, directions and cultural activities in this capital city. "I absolutely love what I do," she answers when asked about whether she enjoys her work. "I get to meet people from all over the world, get exposed to new cultures and help those people enjoy my country."

Gloria didn't start out in Quito. Like many residents, she immigrated from a smaller village. "I grew up in the north of Ecuador, in a small village near the border with Colombia. After I finished high school, my mother basically pushed me out to the city...I came to look for new opportunities. Both she and I knew that if I stayed in our small village there would be nothing to do." Gloria's mother wanted all of her four children to have a different life than she had and encouraged them all to leave for new opportunities, including her oldest sister who now lives in the United States, her next older sister who is a teacher in Quito and her younger brother.

"If I stayed there, for sure I would have gotten married early and had five kids maybe," she says with a playful laugh. Gloria is not married and has no children, which is unusual for Ecuador. "When I turned 30, some people joked that now I was in the group called 'Vestir Santos' (Dress as Saints) – Whose only purpose was to dress saintly and go to church; that was not for me!" Both men and women tend to marry very young in most of Latin America, with most girls dreaming of a lavish church wedding, parading down the aisle all in white. Not Gloria. "Even when I was young, I didn't want the dream of a big wedding, it wasn't for me."

Another area where Gloria differs from her peers is religious practices. "I am Catholic and have faith, but I have major problems with the church. I have become alienated because of its atrocious past and present as an instrument of oppression, especially with women. Women are relegated to second class churchgoers. Being women, we can not aspire at the very least to be a priest, far less archbishops, cardinals and more than impossible, to become a pope."

When asked about the idea of getting married and someday having children, she says it is still a possibility. "I would like to be with someone, but I don't feel like I have to get married. Children could be nice but I don't think I am brave enough to be a single mom. You have to be brave here. In Ecuador you get no support from the state; if you don't have family helping you with maternity leave or child care, it is very, very hard." However, after speaking with Gloria and watching her confidence, it seems hard to believe she would not be brave enough for any task.

At age 30, Gloria summoned her courage and traveled alone to Europe for three months, spending part of the time with friends in Italy, but making the journey solo. Her trip was definitely not the norm for her economic level – she considers herself a little less than middle class. "My mother was a housekeeper and my dad was a farmer, so making a trip like this was a big deal." The trip was her first experience out of Ecuador and first time on an airplane and she loved it.

"Even though I was nervous and didn't sleep for two nights before leaving and was scared every time I had to take the train, it was an amazing experience."

Although she was apprehensive, Gloria found she met wonderful people everywhere I went. "Everything you give, you receive... Maybe it was because I had been in the hotel business for almost 15 years at that point and I helped so many people, but I was surprised people were so kind." Five years later she returned to Italy to again visit friends and see more of the country. Three years ago she traveled to Bolivia to learn more about native Indian cultures and explore her own heritage. "I realized on that trip we are all who we are, bits and pieces of everything."

Through her travels Gloria also gained the realization that she doesn't have to be a doctor or engineer to learn how to be an empowered individual, sure of her rights and her freedoms as a woman and as a citizen. "In a patriarchal and closed-minded society as the Ecuadorian one, I feel this is a great accomplishment and therefore, one of my proudest achievements is to make my family and friends proud of me – this is my small contribution to my country."

As she approaches 40, the number itself is not a big number in Ecuador. "More people here celebrate turning 50 – a half-century – it's a bigger deal." When she was 25, each year older was dreaded a bit; the comment was always "oh, another year…" Since turning 38 Gloria finds she doesn't worry about the number on the calendar. "I remember reading last year Ricky Martin was 40 and I realized he was older than me and I still had another year until I had to even think about being 39; it made me laugh!"

"I have a friend who says when we arrive at 40, we start to question what we have done and what we are going to do now, to look back and forward. There was a period when I started to doubt if I had done anything. Now, I know, I have done a lot. I speak many languages. I am interested in many things, I have done a lot. At 40 I expect to be more sure of my decisions and more sure of myself." She tries not to think too hard about far-off future plans but instead to live more in the moment. "Who knows where I will be in 10 years? I would love to have my own hotel some day, with me out front taking care of everyone, sharing all that I love about my country."

One aspect of turning 40 Gloria looks forward to is being more confident in her decisions and direction. "When I was 30, I was still looking for me….Now I feel like I have found myself. My older sister doesn't agree though – she says that we never actually *find* ourselves, we are always still looking for ourselves."

- **Biggest Accomplishment**: My solo trip to Europe and visiting the United States, including Washington, Oregon and New York.

- **Biggest Regret**: Not finishing my college degree. I went to a Polytechnic University for 2 ½ years to learn English but left for my first hotel job and never went back. I know I could finish now if I wanted, I just need a push to get going!

⚞ *Biggest Surprise at 40*: I am surprised at my capacity to continue – To not give up. I am stronger than I expected. I am also always surprised at people and their capacity to be generous and to change the world. We have had really bad moments here in Ecuador, and now we are living in a good moment; it surprises me. Five years ago I thought maybe I would leave Ecuador if the political situation did not improve. But now, we are working for a change.

⚞ *What Would you Change if you Could?* I would like to have had a common adolescence. Mine was not common because my mom got arthritis when I was 8 -- It marked our lives. It was very aggressive and painful. I was only 8, but I was also now a helper in the house. I was like a mini-mom. I had an adolescence living like a grown up. It was the same for my older sister – It was one of the reasons why she didn't have kids – 'I already raised my kids, why do I want more?' It was hard work. I wanted good grades and helped with the house, so I didn't party with friends, or have a boyfriend, etc. – I postponed until later to do fun things.

⚞ *What Would You Do With an Extra $100?* I would spend it! If I have to save I save. I might have regrets after, but I would probably spend it – Probably on something for the house, then something for me – Maybe a pair of shoes. *With an Extra $1,000?* I would save most of it -- $800. Would spend $200. *An Extra $10,000?* The same, I would save most of it, Maybe spend a few hundred dollars. Would want to save all of it.

Guida

Torino, Italy

"Being 40, it's dawned on me – If you want to do something, this is the time to do it!

Guida is not Italian by birth, rather by choice. This is evident as I meet her at her apartment in Torino where she has made a lovely spread of appertivo (happy hour) food choices and a bubbly Prosecco to sip on. Born and raised by parents who immigrated from the Island of Madeira to South Africa, she spent her childhood in a country setting outside Johannesburg with lots of land, a large house – but in an entirely segregated nation. She lived in a time where blacks were officially second class citizens (or less) but in many mays she was sheltered from a lot of the hatred of apartheid. "I really wasn't aware how separated our lives were from everyone else."

Her father found himself in South Africa after a coup in Mozambique forced him to relocate (her mother had been living Madeira). "I almost didn't exist," she adds with a smile. "My father went to Madeira and fell in love with my mother while she was in a convent. In her 20s she left and married my father at 33. They moved back to South Africa where I was born." She speaks fondly of growing up at a time where, as a white person, you had many privileges and a bit of a charmed life. "It was a happy life," she says.

After attending high school and university in South Africa, Guida dreamed of a change. "I decided to take a gap year and wanted to work as an Au Pair and see more of the world. I applied with families in France and Italy and I got a dream assignment – A model from Milan needed someone to travel with her family and new baby as she worked in Paris, Milan and New York. I was so excited!" This type of adventure was exactly what she was seeking. Guida accepted the job and prepared to relocate the beginning of the next year. In October, just a few weeks before she was to leave for this assignment, came a new call. Her agency told her of a family based in Torino with a young child that wanted a South African Au Pair based on their previous success with a girl from the same country. "Was my dream of France out the window?" she wondered.

"I had to make a choice...I didn't even know where Torino was; I had to look at a map! This was before the internet was everywhere and I actually pulled out an old-fashioned atlas!" As it turns out, the outgoing South African Au Pair had a wonderful experience with the family and called Guida to speak to her about the assignment. The family called her as well to get to know her a bit and try and convince her to make the choice. "I decided that if I was going to make this big move for a year, I wanted it to have meaning, I wanted to be part of a family, not just a babysitter."

Guida made the choice to come to Torino and has not regretted it. "The family was absolutely wonderful, treating me like a daughter. We shared many happy moments and I got to travel with them – to both Milan and Paris. I still haven't been to New York – not yet!" she adds with a giggle.

Towards the end of that first year, she had built a friendship with a local Italian man who would end up playing an important part of her life. "After the one-year assignment was over, I left and returned to South African to be with friends and family. Then, something very strange happened – I realized I didn't belong there any more." You can see the heartbreak in her face when she discusses the time in her life where she realized the home she thought was so ideal wasn't so much so anymore. "I grew up in such a segregated country, where everyone was very limited. When I came to Torino, I felt like my eyes had been opened in so many ways and I felt so free. We had a huge parcel of land at home and a nice big house but I wasn't free. In Italy, I had a very small apartment surrounded by thousands of people but I felt free."

Guida's thinking and way of life had changed forever. She decided to return to Torino for another six-month Au Pair assignment. During that time period, her friendship with the Italian man forged during her first assignment blossomed into a full-blown romance. The two dated for three years and married when Guida was 26. "He's definitely Italian, born and bred, a man of the south," she laughs. His parents are from southern Italy and her husband is quite close to them. She speaks honestly about gaining a mother-in-law with very different cultural values than her own and trying to win her approval. "In Italy, mothers never think any other woman is good enough for their son."

While she was happy with her decision to remain in Italy and become married, she acknowledges there have been challenges on many levels. "Italian women, while friendly, are not necessarily anxious to take you in to their circle of friends. Many of them were born and raised together and have their circles well established. As an outsider, it can be difficult to join in. "Most of my friends are other expats, living in Italy but from other countries," she says. Guida speaks of her best friend in Torino who recently has made the decision to relocate back home to Australia after a breakup. "It's hard, I am really sad," she says. "I don't know what I am going to do without her."

One way Guida has integrated successfully in Torino is through work. "When I first came here after finishing as an Au Pair I had a degree in communication but it was hard to get work because I wasn't fluent in Italian. Back then, English wasn't really important. I ended up at a local school seeking Italian lessons and they wanted to know if I was a native English speaker – they needed someone for an English language conversational class." This was a path Guida hadn't even considered. "But I am not a teacher, don't have any training in instruction," she said. It didn't matter, they just needed speakers for the conversational class. "So I taught a class. Then

another, then another. By the end of the month, I was teaching 25 hours. I guess you could say I became a teacher by chance!" She traveled to London to complete her coursework to receive her ESL (English as a Second Language) instruction certification and she was off on her new career.

"As I worked, I realized there were not any classes for 'business English' – instructing people on how to lead presentations, make sales calls, etc. I approached the school and said I could start offering classes in this area. It became very popular. 17 years ago this was an entirely new concept. Now, I work almost entirely with businesses leading courses on 'business English' and training professionals in the art of negotiation. I love it!" While the pay is not that great, she wouldn't change a thing. "I love my job and get to work with so many people. There's not one day that I get up where I don't want to go to work."

Her son Christopher also brings a smile to her face each day. "We waited quite a long time before having a child...I guess you could say we had a bit of the 'Seven-Year Itch,'" she says. The couple actually split up for a while but then decided to reconnect and continue their marriage. Christoper's birth in 2007 has been a great joy and also has helped soothe some of the tensions with her Italian mother-in-law, giving them a grandchild to dote on.

"When I was growing up in South Africa, I pictured myself as an adult living in suburbia, dropping my kids at school, being active in the parent's association – the way I grew up. I never thought I would be here, but I don't wish anything different, just wish it was a little easier with the cultural and family adjustments." Guida's sadness about being far away from her family as her son grows up is evident as she speaks. "They can't see him change every day – We see them once a year and to him they are just people on the phone or computer screen; he doesn't know them." They do see her husband's family much more often and her in-laws are very close to her son. "Once Christopher came along, everything seemed to be OK. Now, my mother-in-law is my lifesaver. She picks him up every day after school and will watch him in the afternoons – sometimes even making me some dinner so I have something when I am home from work!" We sample her mother-in-law's scrumptious signature vegetable torte as we talk.

When asked about having more children, she does confess that she did at one time dream of having another, but now she just doesn't see it coming. "The economy is so bad here in Europe and both my husband and his family recently had to close their businesses." Now working on a contract basis in the IT industry, she admits her husband's career at this point is probably not stable enough to support another child. "It wouldn't be a smart thing to have another child – I'd want to provide the best for them in schooling, etc. and I don't think it's possible now. It's not a nice thing to say the economy can dictate your family choices, but it's something we have to think about."

Previously, Guida had dreamed of taking her family (perhaps with additional children) back to her native South Africa. She realizes now this just isn't possible. Her parents left South Africa for good in 2001, returning to their native Madeira. After being attacked or carjacked five times, her father had enough. Her sister too. "She was also carjacked and has since moved on to London." Her one brother remains in South Africa, running a business and takes the attitude of "where else am I going to go? My life is here." Now, if she moved back, she thinks she would be scared. Even though apartheid is over, it is a lot more violent. "People are no longer officially segregated but it seems like everyone voluntarily segregates themselves. You can't go out, it's not free. Everyone has a horror story to tell you and it's not where I want my child to grow up. Even though I miss my space, I value my freedom here more."

"If I could change anything, it would be to live closer to my family. I used to think I wanted to bring my son up the way I was raised. I only realized later once I came abroad that the nice way of life I had was just for white people. Now though, it is too frightening. I would probably segregate him just because I was afraid. Once you go back there, you find yourself getting scared and that really bothers me. You are suspicious of every person even if you don't want to be." Her always-smiling face turns sad and her voice a tad melancholy. "People just won't understand until they live there. It humbled me coming here and seeing how different life can be."

Now at 40 and truly settled in her life in Torino, Guida wants more for the future. "I would really like to create something, something that I have contributed to make people happy. I've had this idea in my drawer for years, it's the Pisces side of me that wants to be creative. I'm working on a signature souvenir item for the island of Madeira where my parents are. Being 40, it's dawned on me – this is it, Guida, time to do it!"

- *Biggest Accomplishment*: Learning a new language, living in a new culture, becoming a mother, running a marathon. I consider these all just little accomplishments but they build on the person I am today. I know that living them every day makes me want to do more.

- *Biggest Regret*: I try not to think about regrets. For me, a regret is maybe just a learning experience; you have to just learn from it instead. The moment you make a decision, you can't regret, you can just learn from it.

- *Biggest Surprise at 40*: That I am 40 but feel 22!

- *What Would you Change if you Could?* I wish I could be closer to my family.

- *What Would You Do With an Extra $100?* Go out for a nice meal with my family. *With an Extra $1,000?* Book a short holiday. *An Extra $10,000?* Invest it.

Julie

Brussels, Belgium
"I left a lucrative career to leap into the unknown...am I nuts?"

Julie knows a thing or two about pressure. As a former partner in a major international law firm, she was used to deadlines, client demands and expectations to win multi-million dollar judgments. After 14 years of burning the candle at both ends Julie has hung up her legal briefs and is embarking on a new adventure, except she just doesn't know what it is yet. Years of long hours, grueling workload and lifestyle sacrifices led her to review her career choice and seek something new. "My life had become far too one-dimensional and it was time to put more of my energy into other interests."

During one particularly brutal case several years ago, she realized this was no way to live. She was basically living out of a temporary office space and a federal courthouse 3,000 miles from her home in Los Angeles for two solid months, heading to a hotel room for a few hours to sleep each night. After that, it was a whirlwind 31-hour business trip to Asia -- 24 hours of flying time, 7 hours on the ground; there wasn't even time for her body to try to adjust to a new time zone.

She was making far more money than many of her friends in the same age bracket, but she had almost no time to stop and enjoy it. Additionally, the allure of living in Los Angeles had worn off and was no longer something with which she identified. She knew she needed a change of scenery, but didn't have a destination in mind.

She wouldn't have guessed she would be starting her new life in the land of chocolates, beer, frites and waffles -- Belgium. The former California resident moved to the European capital city of Brussels almost six years ago for a work assignment and it's been home ever since. Her career afforded her the opportunity to enjoy the finest parts of living on the continent, including delicious food, wine and weekend trips to France, Italy and the Greek Islands. Now, she is transitioning out of a power-position lifestyle into one more reflective and creative, and definitely less certain. She's embarking on a new career as she approaches 40 as a professional photographer and writer.

"I'm not as worried about turning 40 as I was about turning 29. As my 29th birthday approached I felt tired and old. It seemed that all I had done was go to school and burn long hours at work. I had very little to show for it. By the time I turned 30, I was feeling more accomplished after purchasing my own home and doing more independent travel. I knew then (10 years ago) that I wanted more than one career in my lifetime, so I set a goal of leaving law before I was 40. I left a few weeks shy of my 39th birthday, so mission accomplished."

She's now using money she saved during her previous legal career to fund this next chapter in her life. It hasn't been an entirely smooth process, however. "Not everyone in my inner circle understood this change. Some couldn't grasp the concept of giving up a high-paid, comfortable position in the legal industry for one of uncertainty; some thought I was leaping off a cliff." Undaunted, Julie is making that leap and has chosen to stay in her new adopted home of Belgium with her boyfriend of two and a half years, rather than return to the United States. "Until recently, we were both breadwinners and now, during this new phase in my life, he's the primary breadwinner. It's definitely new territory for me."

If you asked Julie at 30 or 35 what she thought her life at 40 would be, she would have expected to be making the career switch she mapped out for herself, but would never have thought it would have been 5,600 miles from then home in Los Angeles. "I knew I would be on a journey, but had no idea what the transition would be or where (geographically) I might end up."

While she works on figuring out her career path post-law, she also needs to map out what else she wants to accomplish personally.

"For so many years my career was the driving factor in almost every decision I made. With that element removed, I have more time to think about what I actually *want* versus what I am *compelled* to do. It's a scary thought in many ways."

High on the list is moving forward regarding marriage and kids. She and her boyfriend have no firm plans yet to marry, although they have both agreed this is the next logical step. Julie knows that her chances for children might be challenging as she was dominated by her career for so long, but feels there is no need to dwell on "what-ifs."

Looking forward from 40, Julie realizes there are so many things she still doesn't know, both about herself and the world around her. "I'm finding new things out every day, and I used to naively think that I would have a better handle on more things by now...I guess there's still much more journey to come."

Update: As this book was going to press, Julie was celebrating her first wedding anniversary with Stephen. They are expecting their first child in a few months, shortly after Julie's 41st birthday. She is now working as a child and family photographer in Brussels and enjoying sharing in some of the positive and happy times in her clients' lives, rather than the challenging/adverse ones that generally caused her legal clients to seek her out.

- *What is your most prized possession (excluding children/people?)*: My senses (vision, hearing, smelling and tasting) for they allow me to experience the world fully and to savor my daily life and the unique nuances of the places I get to visit.

- *Biggest Accomplishment:* Having and maintaining a network of close friends around the globe; life would not be anywhere near as sweet without them and I cherish our times together.

- *Biggest Regret:* I don't really believe in regrets, but I do wish I had known my grandparents better.

- *Biggest Surprise at 40:* That I don't miss anything about a career that dominated my life for so many years.

- *What Would you Change if you Could?* I wish I was a more naturally talented linguist; it's hard living in a country where your native tongue is not the local language!

- *What Would You Do With an Extra $100?* Splurge on a massage. *With an Extra $1,000?* Plan a romantic weekend away. *An Extra $10,000?* Take a multi-month trip to South America or Bhutan & Tibet.

Julie

Washington DC, USA

"I like the idea of using power for good."

What makes a high-powered political fundraiser, used to rubbing elbows with Washington's power elite, decide to step aside from the highest-paying clients and seek those of the more four-legged variety? For Capitol Hill insider Julie, it was an opportunity to use her skills and expertise for a different purpose. "I really believe everything happens for a reason, and when Stout came into my life, it helped me get on a pretty different path from where I was." Stout is her seven-year-old adopted Rottweiler that now goes almost everywhere she does.

Julie went to college at American University and began working as a researcher. She came to Washington because she loved politics and as a child she often thought she would either be a lawyer...or a veterinarian. It's funny how her life has come full circle. "I knew a research job wasn't for me

almost immediately, I am much more of a people person and love the interaction."
After graduation she got a job with a Republican fundraising firm, and from there she
took off like a rocket.

"I was just a kid working directly with U.S. Senators at that first job. I was forced to
learn on the fly and got good at fundraising pretty quickly; I found I really had a
knack for it." She found herself cold-calling millionaires and business leaders,
soliciting funds for various Republican candidates. "Money never stops. Money
never ends in this town. It's just part of the process...It's a hard part of the process,
but important."

After a few years Julie started her own
political fundraising firm ("I wish I had
done it sooner!" she comments). She
eventually also got her master's degree in
political management but never did go to
law school. She regrets this a bit, but
realizes there wasn't really a need for it in
her career and also no longer thought she
had enough time. "I would look at my life
and as I was getting older, I thought – it's
too late! But then I also realized I was
doing everything I would have done
anyway, with or without the law degree."

A few years ago Julie realized she was just
burned out. "I wasn't really enjoying work
as much any more and I was definitely tired
of the 24/7 lifestyle that comes with
fundraising for political candidates." A
friend had gotten her involved with the
Washington DC Humane Society and she

started fostering dogs. At one time she provided foster care for a litter of seven puppies. "That was by far the hardest work I had ever done – ever." Through her work as a foster pet parent, she came to see the financial needs of the society and realized there was an opportunity to use her valuable experience in political fundraising for another purpose.

Now, the Washington DC Humane Society is a client and she is getting ready to launch a $25 million capital campaign to help build a new facility and animal welfare campus with the goal of becoming the model humane society in the United States. "I am very excited and honored to be playing an instrumental role in such an important endeavor. Everyone always wonders if they will leave a legacy – I hope to make this one mine."

Working on Capitol Hill has been interesting on the personal front, as well. Julie's partner of seven years Kathryn is an attorney and lobbyist and the two have gone through some challenging experiences as a couple. Several years ago, Kathryn served as counsel on the Judiciary Committee with it passed the Defense of Marriage Act, severely limiting gay rights. As an openly gay woman, she took a lot of flack from friends and colleagues that couldn't understand how she could work on something that directly negatively impacted her own rights. "We both try to separate work from our personal lives," said Julie. Even though they are Republicans themselves, they often find themselves on the other side of the fence from their co-workers or even their bosses when it comes to some issues, but Julie feels like there are opportunities to advocate for change. "Often, you can get a lot more done from the inside than out."

Julie's partner is now doing just that, working at a law firm and has agreed to be the lead Republican looking to repeal the Defense of Marriage Act. "I know that my co-workers and friends often have to vote a certain way based on their constituents, but I don't take it personally. I know the people who know me and love me could care less that I am gay; they'd never do anything to personally hurt us or disrespect us."

Julie and Kathryn don't plan to marry, since they technically live in Virginia, where gay marriage is not legal, even though it is legal in Washington DC.

In the coming years, Julie hopes to continue to manage fundraising campaigns for clients, but hopefully transitioning to more time in her Florida office to escape the East Coast winters. "I want to continue to strike a balance between my political clients and my non-profits projects, and be passionate about what I am doing – life is too short to just go through the motions!"

- **Biggest Accomplishment**: I think my biggest accomplishment is having found a way to translate my nearly 20 years of political fundraising experience into helping a cause I am very passionate about.

- **Biggest Regret**: Not going to law school.

- **Biggest Surprise at 40**: I think the biggest surprise is that I have my own company and am pretty content with all that I am doing. When I was younger I was always looking for "something else," but I think I have finally found my niche.

- **What Would you Change if you Could?** I would have started my own company sooner!

- **What Would You Do With an Extra $100?** Spend it on regular expenses. **With an Extra $1,000?** Put it in savings. **An Extra $10,000?** Save some and donate some.

Kristin

Washington DC, USA

"When I came to DC I was kind of a hippie – It's funny where life takes you"

You can't really say Kristin fell into her political life as Chief of Staff for a Congressman on Washington DC's Capitol Hill. She's been at it for a while, but it's not really where she thought she would be.

Moving to the capital after studying environmental and Indian law at the University of Colorado, she came to the political heart of the country to work as an advocate. She studied environmental law, water and land rights, so Kristin was confident she would work outside the mainstream DC circle, battling to be heard.

"I didn't expect to actually be *in* government, I thought I would be advocating *to* government," she says. Her first job was a legislative aide for a Congressman and after a few years learning the ropes, she realized she was better suited for a career focused on many issues, not just a single cause. "Working on staff you get to do a little bit of everything and it never gets boring, which I like...I figured out I'm better as a multi-tasker." She's also learned that you can advocate for change while working within the system. As Chief of Staff for Congressman Jim Langevin of Rhode Island, she oversees the legislative staff, consults with her boss, sits in committee meetings and helps direct policy decisions.

When Kristin first interviewed with the Congressman in 2000 just after his election to the House, they clicked almost immediately on writing styles and outlook on government. "My voice really seemed to match his and I felt we could work well together and help effect change." She had never even been to the Congressman's home state of Rhode Island before she got hired.

As Chief of Staff, she is basically Langevin's right hand, managing his agenda, schedule and advisers. Unlike other Chiefs on the Hill, Kristin has additional duties with her boss. Congressman Langevin has been in a wheelchair for over 30 years, paralyzed from the waist down after an accidental shooting while volunteering at a local police department. "It adds a whole other layer to the job," Kristin says. "At every event, every appointment, I have to be aware of his needs, whether it be writing things down, assisting with food and drinks or even just standing over his shoulder to help him clear papers and files." When her contemporaries might be able to rest for a few minutes during an event knowing their boss is comfortably schmoozing, Kristin needs to stay attentive to ensure no intrusions from Langevin's disability interfere with his work.

What's truly amazing is that the buildings the Congressman works in, The Cannon Building and The U.S. Capitol, are not entirely ADA (Americans with Disabilities Act) compliant. When Kristin and the Congressman came to the hill, it became obvious that part of their job would be to make the landmarks more accessible for everyone – not just members, but visitors and office workers as well. "Besides all of the work we do on a daily basis on our regular policy items, we are always pushing the accessibility agenda." Since beginning his tenure, the Congressman and his staff have had several committee rooms and even the House Floor modified to accommodate Langevin's wheelchair.

Serving as a Chief of Staff is not unheard of for a woman in DC, but it is still not the norm and working mom chiefs are fairly uncommon. Kristin and her husband have two young boys, Ian (5) and Alec (2). Her hectic schedule made tending for her very young children challenging, especially while nursing. "It was a bit of a circus," Kristin says and laughs. "Luckily, I had a good friend who had each of her two children around the same time I had mine...We would step out discreetly together and find a quiet place if we needed to pump during the day. Sometimes we'd find a spot in the nurse's office and turn on C-SPAN while pumping to ensure we didn't miss out on any conversations on the floor...I even had to take my breast pump with me to an aircraft carrier off the coast of San Diego when we went for a one-night visit with the troops. Talking to a 19-year old naval officer about finding a private spot to pump was pretty hilarious!" You can tell Kristin goes with the flow and loves the diversity of her job, even if it includes a bit of a juggling act.

After working in the political arena for nearly 15 years now and seeing what it takes to be an effective elected leader, Kristin has no interest in ever pursuing a career in the public eye. "I'm just not that much of a networker, and don't have that 'thing' – that ability to come into a room, talk to everyone and make small talk on any number of subjects. It's not for me, I'd rather be behind the scenes." She does have a large network of friends and associates in the DC area, many of which work in politics, when she needs to bounce ideas around or discuss work issues.

Now approaching 40, Kristin is confident and comfortable in her own skin. When she was younger she felt like she was "playing catch up" to a lot of her older co-workers and friends since she was young for her class and started off fairly aggressively in her career immediately after law school. Her immediate circle of friends are mostly 40 or just approaching 40; however, her co-workers, with whom she spends most of her time, are mostly in their 20's and early 30's. "I think people would be surprised at how many young people are in positions of power in DC. The number of 20-somethings running the Hill is truly staggering!"

In her own younger years working in DC, Kristin had a completely different off-work persona: Hip-hop DJ. Upon arriving in the city, she had a number of friends with clubs and bars who knew about Kristin's lifelong passion for music. She loves all types and found she had a real knack for DJ'ing, especially hip hop. It wasn't uncommon to find her at some of the most notable clubs in the city spinning tunes until the wee hours of the morning...Until her first son came along. "When I became a mom I knew I had to cut back on the DJ gigs, but it's a part of my life I'm glad I did; I was even named in *Washingtonian Magazine* as an up-and-coming DJ to watch. Sadly, that part of their magazine archive is now off their web site, and my Google search is much more boring today!"

- *Biggest Accomplishment*: I am very proud of the career I've built, and even more proud that I've managed to continue my professional success while also raising two amazing children, cultivating a strong marriage, creating a home that I love, playing volunteer roles at both children's schools and maintaining close friendships with many great people from all areas of my life.

- *Biggest Regret*: I honestly can't think of any major disappointments or regrets.

- *Biggest Surprise at 40*: The biggest surprise is that I am the mother of two boys –

and I actually love it! I am the only child who grew up largely with a single mom, and I never imagined anything other than having girls.

⚔ *What Would you Change if you Could?* I would love to have the opportunity to live abroad for a year or two, but the work that my husband and I do is so tied to DC, it's never been a realistic option. That, and I've never been much of a risk-taker. I also wish that my parents lived closer to me so that my kids could spend more time with them.

⚔ *What Would You Do With an Extra $100?*   Splurge on a nice meal or a piece of clothing. *With an Extra $1,000?*   Go away for the weekend away with my husband. *An Extra $10,000?*   Put it in savings or toward a household project.

Mala

Edapady, India

"I want to be healthy and financially strong to take care of my kids."

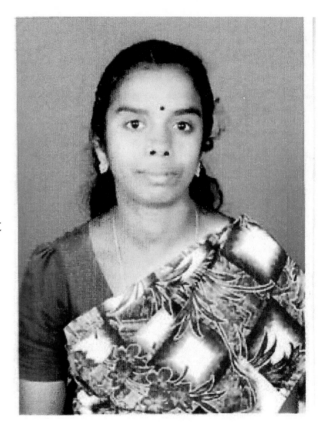

Just a few months short of her 40th birthday, Mala is a widow facing an uncertain future. About 10 years ago, she received devastating news: She had HIV. She was diagnosed after her husband became ill and was determined to be sick with AIDS.

We interviewed Mala via email and remote phone calls thanks to our charity partner, Project Concern International (www.pciglobal.org). Over the past decade, PCI/India has managed and implemented approximately 30 programs that expand HIV/AIDS prevention and care and support among high-risk groups and their families in urban and peri-urban slums, as well as build and strengthen the networks of PLHIV at the local, state and national levels. Specifically, between 2003 and 2009, PCI in partnership with the US Centers for Disease Control and Prevention (CDC), built and managed the most extensive and comprehensive HIV community and home-based care (CHBC) program in the country, delivering services to an estimated 6,000 direct beneficiaries annually in five high-prevalence states.

When she was diagnosed, her two sons were very young, just one and three years old.

Her husband did not live long past his diagnosis. Mala was lost; however, she found some hope. "Soon after the demise of my husband, I was introduced to the PATHWAY program and I became a Peer Educator. This program equipped me with training and skills which helped me in getting employment even after I completed PATHWAY and I have been able to support my family for the last 10 years."

She now works as a Field Staff member for the Don Bosco NGO (Non-Governmental Organization). In her position, she interacts with HIV-positive children. Even though she has a job, she considers herself to be struggling – "to meet the growing expenses of the family; I have been supporting my family all alone."

Shortly after Mala was married her mother died; then she lost her husband. After his death she also lost her only brother. "If I did not have my children I could have ended my life." Again though, she remains hopeful: "The PATHAWAY program helped me in supporting a number of women and children like me in the community," she says.

Part of that aloneness is a hard fact: "I am worried about the future of my children; nobody is there to take of my children. My husband, parents and siblings are no more." Who will take care of her children if Mala does not live long enough to see them grown and with families of their own? This is a hard fact many of the women we have encountered in this project have probably not had to think about when it comes to turning 40. Mala is hoping to just make it to 40, and beyond at least a few years.

"When I thought about being 40, I thought it would be normal and I would be happy with my kids and husband. Due to HIV my future has become dark and I am really worried about the future of my children." When asked about looking ahead to 50, her answer is very pragmatic: "I want to be healthy and financially strong to take care of my kids."

- *Biggest Accomplishment*: That I have been able to support my family all alone.

- *Biggest Regret*: If I didn't have my children I would probably have ended my life.

- *Biggest Surprise at 40*: Alas, I can't imagine the twist and turns in my life.

- *What Would You Do With an Extra $100?* Invest in my small provisional store to earn more. *With an Extra $1,000?* Provide good and quality education to my children. *An Extra $10,000?* Make a fixed deposit in the name of my children for their bright future.

Marcella

Tijuana, Mexico
"I thought turning 40 would be terrible...It was not!"

Tijuana, Mexico is not an easy place to live. Crowds, traffic, pollution and unending border waits have been aggravated in recent years with a dramatic acceleration in drug violence throughout the country. Marcella has lived almost her entire life in this border town and has watched it change... unfortunately, for the worse. "When I was younger, my husband and I would go out all the time. Sometimes I would drive home late at night by myself with my top down in my Jeep; I wasn't afraid." Marcella has reason to be afraid now.

Just four days before our interview, a San Diego-born teenager was convicted of homicide and organized crime charges in the beheadings of four men on behalf of a drug cartel in central Mexico. The August 2010 killings ended with mutilated bodies being strung from a highway bridge in Cuernavaca, a tourist destination just south of Mexico City. In the first 7 months of 2011 alone, Tijuana saw 341 murders, mostly from escalating drug cartel clashes.

Although violence has become a fact of life in this city of approximately 1.8 million, Marcella chooses not to leave, even though she is technically a US citizen. Born in National City, California, just over the border from Mexico, she's lived in Mexico since she was just over a year old. An affordable cost of living and proximity to family is what keeps this mother of two here.

"If we tried to live in California, we wouldn't have very much money, we wouldn't be able to live somewhere nice." In Tijuana, Marcella and her husband and their two daughters live in an apartment attached to her mother's home.

Marcella did not finish high school – she went to elementary and middle school in Tijuana and then attempted to complete high school via Adult School in San Diego County, but she chose not to complete her coursework. "I began working and saw that I could make more money the more I worked, so I did not finish." After getting married, she worked for nine years at a JCPenney store in San Diego, commuting across the border several times a week. Crossing between Mexico and the United States is a brutal fact of life for those that live a cross-border existence in this part of the country.

Marcella's husband currently works full time in San Diego at a local ship builder supporting the region's Navy presence and commutes either via trolley (about 1 hour each way) or car (can vary between 1 and 3 hours each way, depending on traffic). She misses some of the extra income that her retail job generated and the shopping sprees for clothes and cosmetics, but she confesses that "things are better now – I am spending the money we do have on things that matter the most, like my daughters and our home; it forces me to see what is important."

At age 38 Marcella decided to take some of the money she would have spent on shopping and use it to make the most of one of Mexico's economic advantages: Reduced prices on major medical procedures. She elected to have a variation of gastric bypass surgery called "Manga Elastica" and lost 135 pounds. She spent a fraction of the usual $20,000 – $30,000 this procedure can cost in the United States. "I didn't want to be 40 and fat and unhealthy," she adds. Even with complications from the procedure and additional hospitalization to treat a kidney infection, she would still do it again.

Now at 40, Marcella feels like she is much healthier than before and wants the best for her daughters, age 11 and 6. However, she acknowledges the Tijuana they are growing up in is far different from the one she remembers as a child. Nearly 80% of all classroom instruction is in English; Spanish is almost becoming a second language here, and in some cases, almost a caricature of itself. "I watch television commercials out of the United States aimed at Mexicans and I can't believe how bad the horrible the accents are and the outfits they make actors wear – it looks fake." One of our other guests at lunch comments that one of her nephews speaks nothing but English and his grandmother speaks nothing but Spanish; the two have created their own mash-up language to communicate with each other.

What's in the future for Marcella? She plans to continue as a stay-at-home mom for now in Mexico, being available for her kids. As they get older, she will consider possibly going back to school to become a medical assistant and maybe relocating back to the United States. "Who knows?" she comments with a glimmer in her eye. She stops, lets out an infectious, bubbly laugh and says "I was afraid I wouldn't be a good mom and that has worked out OK, so we'll see!"

- **Biggest Accomplishment:** My daughters.

- **Biggest Regret:** Sometimes I have to be very tough on my oldest daughter to get her to study; she doesn't do well unless I am hard on her and I don't like it.

- **Biggest Surprise at 40:** I don't feel any different than I did at 39; I tried Botox because some friends did it and I hated it, I felt like I looked so funny!

- **What Would you Change if you Could?** When I established credit in the United States, I used it to help my sister buy a car...She lost her job and the car got repossessed and it ruined my credit.

- **What Would You Do With an Extra $100?** Go shopping. **With an Extra $1,000?** I guess I am a shopaholic – I would buy something for my daughters. I love to shop, that's one of the reasons I had to quit at JCPenney. **An Extra $10,000?** Fix up my kitchen.

Maria

Brussels, Belgium

"It's not 30, it's not 40, it's not 50...It's that moment that changes your life."

It's easy to see the great joys in Maria's life...Her children. When we meet in a Brussels cafe we start out talking about work, education and her road to Belgium. "My husband and I both joke we came to the city for a short time and somehow lost our return ticket!" However, when the conversation turns to her family and two young daughters aged 3 and 2, her face absolutely lights up.

"When I was 30, I felt like I needed to get serious...It was time to know what I was going to do for the rest of my life. 40 seemed to be a big thing, with lots of things surrounding you. Now though, here at 40, I am so happy, so balanced, happy with my girls and my husband," she says. Maria adds that it wasn't a specific number that changed her life, but rather the moments her children were born. Both Maria and her husband work in Brussels as attorneys and the family has a hectic schedule. "It's a busy life, especially now because the girls are so close in age and are much more vocal and active. I feel like we are busy but it is good – my commute is very short; I leave the office and five minutes later I am with my kids," she adds. I ask her about continuing to work full time and she says "If I can keep on paying them enough attention, then I will keep doing it. I can still take them to school and be with them. When they get older, they will get more demanding for time and attention. I will need to spend more time with them with school and other activities, so that might mean working less.   For the moment, it is working."

That work in Brussels was a natural evolution for Maria. Born and raised in Spain, she studied in her hometown and went to a split Spanish/German school. During her last year of university she was able to study in Germany under a new program designed to encourage cross-cultural studies in Europe. After finishing school and gaining her law license, she felt the most "obvious" thing was to come to Brussels. Like many young career Europeans, Maria journeyed to this capital city for its diverse employment opportunities. "I thought I would stay here maybe six months at the most." She wasn't keen on the city's notoriously dreary weather after growing up in sunny Spain.

Brussels offered other benefits, however. "This is such an international city, it's easy to feel at home here really no matter where you are from," she says. "In other cities you really might have to struggle to acclimate. Here, you can lead your own life depending on your culture; there is a little bit of everything." Like many of her peers, Maria switches easily between French, English, Spanish and German, depending on the situation and company.

Her move from Spain presented another opportunity: Her now husband, Christian, whom she met her first year of work. Both lawyers, he hails from Austria and like Maria came to Brussels for work opportunities. After getting to know each other a bit that first year, they decided to start dating and six years after that were married. "He thought he would get some experience and go back home as well," Maria chuckles. "We found each other and jobs that made us happy, much to the regret of our families!" she laughs. Each very close to their families, they travel frequently to visit and now their two daughters delight to arrive at the airport, knowing they are soon to enjoy family fun in either country.

A recent trip to the United States for a friend's wedding allowed the couple to travel without the girls and celebrate Maria's milestone birthday. "When I looked ahead to 40, I knew I would be with Christian, probably married and assumed I would have a family by then. When you are 30, you look at 40 and you think it's a long way away...50 looks far away when you say "50" psychologically. But when I think how fast the last 10 years went, it's scary, it's closer than you want it to be. In terms of what I wanted to do with life, I think I have done so far what I wanted to do...I don't see myself wanting to be somewhere else other than where I am," she finishes with a smile that makes our corner of the cafe just a little brighter.

Biggest Accomplishment: That I have created a great family and we are so happy. I know though that being happy is so much easier when you can decide what you want to do. If you are unhappy and you have the chance to change things, it's your fault if you don't do it...It's different if it's not your choice. It is much harder to find happiness when you do not have the choice to change things.

⋏ *Biggest Regret*: It's not really a regret, but it is hard being away from the family I grew up with – However, if I hadn't moved to Brussels and started a new life here, I wouldn't have had the family I have now; you can't have one without the other. Still, I wish I could spend even more time with them.

⋏ *Biggest Surprise at 40*: My kids – I really didn't understand this until I had them. You hear people say how much it changes your life, and you can't believe it until it happens to you. Your whole life changes at that moment.

⋏ *What Would you Change if you Could?* I would like to have what I have here closer to Spain -- I would have my family in the sun. If I could, I would move Brussels to Spain and the Austrian mountains closer to Spain as well, it would be perfect! We might move some day for work, but I think for sure we will move at some point when we are no longer working; closer to one family or the other, especially if the girls are off studying somewhere else...there is no point to stay here watching the rain!

⋏ *What Would You Do With an Extra $100?* I'd go for a nice dinner with my friends. *With an Extra $1,000?* I would buy some art – a nice picture probably – for our home. *An Extra $10,000?* I would go for a really nice trip with my family.

Maria

San Diego, California, USA
"I don't feel 40, I feel 20...OK, maybe 30!"

Maria's modest home sits on the eastern outskirts of downtown San Diego. We chat with her in her kitchen as an occasional low hum of an airplane on final approach rumbles overhead. "When I was younger, I didn't really think of my life in the future," she says. "I thought I would probably be married and have children and would maybe go to school." She's a proud mother of four sons aged 20, 18, 17 and 10 and has one infant grandchild. They all live together in the house, along with her son's girlfriend.

The family is almost complete, save one. Last year she sadly lost her husband of 19 years. Although, he wasn't really her husband...they never actually married. "My family really wanted us to marry because of the church, but we never did. We lived together and had our children, but never married." Now, she's on her own, raising her sons and helping to take care of her grandchild. When asked about where she sees herself in the future, she sees a life back in Mexico. "I would love to live in a Ranchito down near Tecate. Maybe when my sons are off and married I would go live there, close to the mountains. Maybe at 50 – that could be nice. My young ones will be grown up and I can go hiking." This is an active mom, one who loves the outdoors and speaks about going hiking as an ideal day.

Moving to Tecate would be a return home for Maria. Born in Mexico, she went to elementary school south of the border, then came to San Diego and only made it as far as the 8th grade. "I lived with my grandmother growing up, not my mother...my grandmother lived here and I was closer to her." Maria never knew her father; he lived in Mexico and she has no idea of his identity or whereabouts. She "married" her husband at 19 and had her first son right away.

Now, she is the primary caretaker of this family of seven and is currently unemployed. Two of her sons work and two are in school; she had been working up until last year in a local hotel but now is without a job. She would like to work again but struggles because of her lack of education. "I wish I had learned more, gotten a skill or career," she adds.

Most of Maria's friends are in her same age bracket, late 30s to early 40s. One of her friends just had a new baby at age 38 and she laughs: "I wouldn't want to do that, I would be too tired...It is hard work taking care of a new baby!" Maria has no plans for any more children at this point in her life and looks forward to family get-togethers and watching her grandchild grow up.

One of those family celebrations will be her pending 40th birthday. However, it won't be marked as any sort of milestone: "It will be just like any other regular birthday, no special party other than anything we would already do --- My grandmother is 85, and when she had her birthday, it was the same as it would be if you were 20, 30 or 40," she says. I ask her if she feels 40: "No, I feel good, I exercise," she says enthusiastically. She had just come from a workout when we met. "I feel like I am 20." She stops for a minute and laughs…"OK, maybe 30!"

- ▲ *Biggest Accomplishment*: Nothing particular comes to mind.

- ▲ *Biggest Regret*:   Not getting an education and feeling ignorant.

- ▲ *Biggest Surprise at 40*:   One of the biggest surprises I had was a Mariachi Band for my birthday – I loved it!

- ▲ *What Would you Change if you Could?* I would have gone to school and gotten a career – I would be interested in a Border Patrol or Police job – I would like to help enforce the law.

- ▲ *What Would You Do With an Extra $100?* Pay bills or buy food. *With an Extra $1,000?* Buy some clothes and save for next month's rent. *An Extra $10,000?* Buy a car…I need a new car and it is so important if you want to have a job, do errands or go to school…I have to go five blocks even to take laundry to the laundromat!

Meghan

Bondurant, Wyoming, USA

"For my 40th birthday, my husband bought me a 270 rifle...I was thrilled; my friends in New York were appalled."

A city girl at heart, Meghan hails from New York. She lived most of her life in Manhattan where there were more people in her subway car on any given morning than in her current hometown of Bondurant, Wyoming (population 100). The road from Wall Street to Sublette County was not a straight ride, especially when it involved a broken down VW bus that eventually led her to her husband and her new life.

Immediately after graduating from Fordham University, Meghan jumped into the tech boom and worked for JP Morgan as an industry analyst. "It was a tremendous time of change and I saw an opportunity, so I started a software business." That move turned out to be quite savvy, as she sold the business just four years later at age 27 and moved to San Francisco to open up the new company's West Coast operations.

After three years of managing the San Francisco office, she decided she needed a change. Using money earned from the sale of her business, she wandered the globe, traveling for almost four years – Meghan explored much of the U.S., South America (living in Argentina for a year), Morocco and then to India. Her U.S. roadtrip included a stop in Jackson Hole, Wyoming for six months...Somehow she knew she would end up returning.

The end of her four-year journey deposited her right back in New York where she found the crowds, noise and people overwhelming, especially after her last stop in an Ashram in southern India. "Everything was so in your face, I realized I had changed and wanted something different."

Even though she knew no one in the area, in 2004 she packed up her 1972 red "Joy" (VW) bus and her dog and drove across country. Jackson Hole was her original destination, but plans, as they are known to do, changed along the way. "The bus broke down on me three times during the drive, the last time was in Yellowstone. I needed a tow to Jackson Hole where I could get the bus fixed. The man who ended up towing my bus later became my husband."

Fast forward seven years. Meghan now has two young sons and a 23-year-old stepson who also lives in Wyoming and she is miles away from where she ever thought she would be. A remote ranching community, 40 miles either way to the nearest towns, is where she calls home. "While Jackson is beautiful, it was not what I thought of as living in Wyoming...our home is much more of a 'Wyoming Place' than the tourist towns nearby."

Breathtaking mountains surround Bondurant, filled mostly with log cabin and ranch-style homes.

"You can't get more different from New York than this. My son is the only kindergartener in a one-room school house that has seven total students." Meghan loves her community and being surrounded by people that made the same conscious choice she did to live in such a rural setting to raise their children.

When asked about the 4-0 milestone, Meghan said that she "didn't feel it was difficult for me, but it definitely made me pause. I went from a solid New York workaholic to a stay-at-home mom in a very rural area. It's never what I would have expected but I love it." She did decide that she needed a bit of a challenge at this point in her life, so she trained for and completed the Big Horn Mountain Wild and Scenic 50 mile ultra trail race, a grueling run through elevation increases and drops through wild back country.

More than the scenery has changed for this onetime city dweller. A former vegetarian, Meghan now hunts deer and elk in the fall. She strives to give her sons a simple and idyllic life, enjoying all that nature has to offer. "We live in a small log cabin, never buy meat from a store, eating only the wild game or fish we have hunted or caught." They use their television only to watch movies; no cable service is hooked up to the house.

"My friends here threw me a party at the only bar in town for my 40th which was great. My husband truly surprised me with a 270 rifle to mark the occasion. I was thrilled; my friends back in New York were appalled. That's how I knew my life was exactly where I wanted it to be."

- **Biggest Accomplishment**: Certainly launching my business at 23 years old and making it a success was my biggest career accomplishment; one day, I hope to repeat that success with another business venture. However, I believe that raising my sons to become successful compassionate men will ultimately be my biggest accomplishment – That is my focus now.

- **Biggest Regret**: I truly do not have any large disappointments or regrets. I have always lived my life the way I have wanted. I believe my family and friends thought it was a bit much sometimes; either they thought I was being reckless or selfish. However, I think they will agree that following my instincts has served me well. Even driving to Wyoming, by myself, not knowing a soul turned out to be one of the best decisions of my life. However, it seemed very questionable at the time.

- **Biggest Surprise at 40**: Having children has certainly been my biggest and most remarkable surprise. I was content working, living in major cities and traveling the world. I did not have the desire that many women have to bear children. However, my husband adores children. He opened my eyes and I am so grateful. Life would have been so boring without them. Only a parent can understand how much they become a part of your being.

- **What Would you Change if you Could?** My husband's work takes him away from home a week at a time. At times it can be hard on our sons. However, when he is at home, we maximize our time together.

- **What Would You Do With an Extra $100?** Get a massage, I never can seem to get enough of them. **With an Extra $1,000?** Travel to the ocean with my husband and sons. The ocean is the only thing I miss living in the mountains. **An Extra $10,000?** Travel to a third world country and stay a month with my husband and sons.

Monica

Las Vegas, Nevada, USA

"I knew what I wanted to do at 13 and have worked to make it happen"

Monica's just a hair outside of our regular 40 year old interviews. However, her story leading up to 40 is one filled with adventures and interesting to share...That, and an incredible love story.

Born and raised in Detroit, Michigan, Monica knew from an early age what she wanted to do. "I remember the actual moment when I knew what I would do for the rest of my life," she says. Monica was attending a private school and it was career day. Her teacher brought in her extremely handsome fiance; the students knew of him through the teacher's comments and photos, but Monica felt there was something else familiar about him. "Once he came in the classroom, I knew instantly where I recognized him from – he did the news on Channel 7. At that moment, I knew what I wanted to do for a living – I wanted to be a news anchor."

From then on, Monica started doing everything she could to hone her skills, including public speaking, presentation and enunciation. She would emcee community events and local fashion shows to practice. Always ready and willing to do whatever it took to get to the next level, she enrolled in a production class for her local TV cable access channel. "We did everything there – shoot events, produce our own stories, host the program. By the time I got to college, I had enough experience to get credit for three classes. It was a bit of a quandary for my professors – How would they teach me things I hadn't already done in real life?" she adds.

At the same time she was beginning her college coursework, she was experiencing life as a new bride. At 18 she married her high school sweetheart, the only man to this day she has ever kissed or even dated. "We were truly like Romeo and Juliet and even now, he gives me butterflies." They eloped to a Justice of the Peace and the light that sparkles in her eyes when she speaks about her husband says volumes. During the first year of their marriage, her husband was stationed in South Korea and Monica stayed behind; they reunited the next year when a transfer brought him to an Air Force base in Utah and Monica finished her coursework there as well.

After Utah Monica's life was nothing but hectic. They relocated back to Michigan where her husband began work as an Air Force Recruiter and she was a blur of motion – Working several part-time and contract jobs in journalism looking for the right fit. "You never know what you can do until it has to be done," she adds when asked about the uncertain nature of this part of her life.

One day she decided she was done with part-time work. She wanted a full-time job in her career of choice. She woke up, put on her best suit, got made up head to toe and slipped on a pair of three-inch heels and stepped into the largest media affiliate office in Detroit, determined to find out what was available. She was hired that day. The cable division had an opening and she took it.

From there she moved on to radio as a Metro Traffic reporter for WCHB-FM. After only two days on the air, the CEO called and asked to meet Monica in person. "Before I knew it, I was on the Morning Breakfast Jam. I'd go home and nap a few hours and then return and do the afternoon traffic on the Reggie Reg show." The exposure was amazing and her career was taking off, but it was also exhausting.

In just under two years, she got another call – this time to join Metro Traffic as a pool traffic reporter in Detroit. "I knew I was close to a big opportunity," she said. Every night, Monica would go to bed with her suit ready and pressed, knowing her big moment was coming. "One night, I got a call from FOX 2. Their traffic reporter had pneumonia and they wanted to know if I could do a live traffic broadcast in-studio. This was my moment; I knew it was my chance." She went to bed with her suit ready for action, shoes shined and makeup already lined up on the counter in advance of her 2:30 a.m. wakeup call.

That moment was the start of her TV career. After just six months, she was recruited away to another station where she worked for four years as an in-studio traffic reporter, but not without a hiccup. "In any career you have your ups and downs...I unfortunately had one big down." After weeks of tension with a newly promoted morning anchor, an off-camera altercation between the two led to Monica's contract not being renewed. "I have a very upbeat and jovial personality, I love to laugh. Sometimes personalities clash, but as an on air personality you have to learn to be professional on and off the camera." Monica would take that experience and became even stronger in her resolve to become a great journalist and on air anchor.

Yet, circumstances seemed to be compounding. In addition to losing her job, Monica's husband had orders to transfer to Las Vegas while her grandmother, who helped raise her and her siblings, was dying of lung cancer in North Carolina. "I see now that not getting my contract renewed was divine intervention. I was able to spend the last few weeks of my grandmother's life with her and I thank God for that time," she adds.

Now, she needed to find a job in Las Vegas. "I refused to believe that the incident at my former job would be the end of my career. I refused to believe God would bring me this far and just drop me." One day she returned home after a temp traffic gig and saw that the FOX affiliate in Las Vegas had an immediate opening for an in-studio traffic reporter. She knew she had to get this job. "The first word on my cover letter was "STOP" in giant letters with multiple exclamation points. 'I am the person for this job, there is nobody in the city that can do traffic better than me. I already have a base here. I am ready to make this happen, are you?' was how I worded the cover letter." She got a call and the News Director wanted her to tell him about herself. She knew it was a test. Monica had nothing to lose so she told the truth – the whole truth – including details of the argument with the former co-worker. "I appreciate your candor, I know the other party involved... I wanted to know if you would tell the truth," he said. She got the job.

Now, six years after being promoted from traffic reporter to FOX5 News morning news anchor, Monica is right where she always knew she would be. "I love the fact that I have a testimony that I can share with other young women trying to get into this business. People tell me that I am lucky – I feel I am blessed that I set out to make that dream came true and it did." Her greatest joy now is the love of her and her husband's lives – their five-year old son. She waited quite a while to become a mom and when asked about more children, she responds with a laugh: "No way! He was nine pounds and we are happy and done!"

It's probably a safe assumption that Monica's ambition is anything but done.

- ⚔ **Biggest Accomplishment**: Giving birth to my son.

- ⚔ **Biggest Regret**: I don't think I have any because all of my challenges have made me the person I am today.

- ⚔ **Biggest Surprise at 40**: The clarity that I have found in my heart, mind and spirit.

- ⚔ **What Would you Change if you Could?** I would change the structure of my professional career so that I could spend more time with my family.

- ⚔ **What Would You Do With an Extra $100?** I'd spend it on my son (for his education or a vacation, etc.) **With an Extra $1,000?** The same. **An Extra $10,000?** The same!

Natalie

New York, New York, USA

"Your heart is your guide...if you relax a little bit and enjoy the ride, you never know where life will take you."

It's 4:15 am and Natalie's alarm clock abruptly signals it's time to get up for work. Like many women, she works in a large group setting...Unlike most women, that group is 6 million people a day. As news anchor on NBC's "The Today Show," Natalie finds herself in a very public arena, delivering vital news and updates to viewers nationwide and around the world thanks to the Internet. She always knew she would be a journalist, but never really imagined her career would take her to The Today Show.

Setting out after getting her degree in journalism, Natalie applied for countless positions in her chosen field, but nothing was available. "This was during the last real recession...No one was hiring, so I made a tough choice to give up on journalism." Natalie was recruited by Chemical Bank for their management training program. "I thought this would be a great opportunity, a fantastic education, basically getting a master's in business while I learned." While the program was educational, Natalie knew this wasn't her intended path. After two years, she resumed her search for a job in her first love of journalism and eventually landed a position at CourtTV. Her new job got her back on the right path; however, it involved taking a 50% pay cut and more uncertainty.

Despite being frightened about the career risk, Natalie was confident. "The move was a very expensive gamble to take, but I knew it would pay off." In the journalism industry, many now-successful reporters speak about having to pay your dues and work your way up, and Natalie was no different. "I kept moving on to better positions and when the opportunity came up at The Today Show, I was thrilled." She knew she had to follow her heart. "Even though you may make mistakes along the way, if you relax a little bit and enjoy the ride, you never know where life will take you," she adds.

That life so far has definitely been an international one, even before landing on The Today Show. Born in Taiwan to a Brazilian mother and a Puerto Rican father, she spent the first 18 years of her life living overseas in Panama, Brazil and Spain as an Air Force 'brat.' Through her work, she has traveled extensively around the world, including covering the Olympics in Athens, Greece and Torino, Italy as well as the Royal Wedding of 2011 in

London and the Chilean Miner Rescue.

One of the best parts about her experiences has been the opportunity to work and live with so many different women around the world. "When you see these other women, you really get to understand the family dynamic. In many cultures, people stay with family until they get married. People really respect their elders. Some of that is lost in our culture." Natalie likes the attitude that many families around the world share about their matriarchs – "You don't get older, you get wiser." Age is not a setback as it sometimes as seen here -- life brings in more experience.

Another difference Natalie sees is the attitude toward work. "People overseas work to live. Here, I think we live to work...there is an importance on how you make a living, and it's too easy to get sucked in and trapped in a sense," she adds. Natalie even sees this in her own life: "I work in a very competitive industry, and sometimes I get caught up in what I do too much – I start thinking 'I should be getting more interviews,' etc. It's great when I travel overseas and I see stories that are more meaningful. I get to see how the rest of the world is living." A famous saying rings true for her: "You always hear that when you are older and wiser, you never will wish you spent more time in the office; it's so true."

Now, as a mom of two young boys, Natalie works to teach her sons the lessons she has learned from around the world and expose them to new cultures. "We might be at home having dinner and I'll tell them to eat up because kids are starving elsewhere, but it's hard for them to grasp." Earlier this year the family was in Rio and after finishing a meal at sidewalk cafe, a young man approached and asked if he could have their leftover pizza. "My son was puzzled and wanted to know why that man wanted our leftover food...I had to explain to him that it was because he was so

hungry he would eat anything, even our leftovers. That really hit home for my son and he could *see* what hunger really is. That's powerful."

Like any working mom, Natalie's day is often a whirlwind juggling act. She's usually at work by 5 am and gets ready for the day by reading countless newspapers, scanning news online, getting details for all her stories of the day. "Fortunately, I have a hair, makeup and wardrobe team to help me get ready for my on-air work each day!" News updates usually start at 6 am and she also preps for any individual news segments in that day's newscast. The live show starts at 7am and runs until 11 am. "The day's not over when we go off the air, though...I have a lot of other stories and things I'm working on for the future so my day is filled with writing, planning, meetings, etc." Natalie tries to squeeze in a one hour window of exercise each day in and then heads home to her family for the most important and sometimes stressful part of the day, being "mom."

She loves to cook and tries to make a home-cooked dinner each night...although it can be a bit challenging. "My boys are picky eaters and my husband doesn't care for fish, so really my go-to meal is chicken...I can do chicken 100 different ways and my husband even calls me the MacGyver of Chicken!," she adds with a laugh. You can tell that despite her high-profile career and busy days, Natalie is just mom to her boys and loves every minute of it.

Part of those crazy days include a regular workout, something Natalie is passionate about. "I've always been a jock, very athletic and competitive," she says. Her latest passion is competing in triathlons after conquering the marathon challenge. "I love running and I have several friends that did triathlons and they encouraged me to try it. I was most nervous about the swim portion, but I found I really enjoy them." Natalie's competed in several different triathlons and is considering the idea of training for a Half-Ironman for her 40th birthday next year. As for the grandaddy of them all, The Ironman? "Someday I would like to do it...I watch our coverage (on NBC) every year from Hawaii and think 'if they can do it I can do it,' so who knows?"

⊁ *Biggest Accomplishment*: Becoming a mom (twice).

- **Biggest Regret**:   I have had regrets and have had a few disappointments, but I think I have learned from each of my life's experiences. I don't like to dwell on what was in the past and focus instead on using what I've learned to keep me from having future regrets. It always seems like there was a plan for me, and I was meant to go down this road no matter whether or not things didn't work out at the time; they have so far in the long run. I'm a big picture person!

- **Biggest Surprise at 40**:   Reaching this level of achievement, though I did have big goals and high expectations for myself.

- **What Would you Change if you Could?**   I wouldn't change much except dwelling on things that are out of my control. I'm all about the journey, not the destination.

- **What Would You Do With an Extra $100?**   Go out to eat. **With an Extra $1,000?** Take a nice trip with my family. **An Extra $10,000?**   Invest it in my kids' college accounts.

Nuria

Lahore, Pakistan

"...Just maybe, my biggest accomplishment is looking at myself and being happy with the person that I have become – which is actually a big deal when one sees that a lot of unhappiness comes from not being happy within."

As much as I would love to interview Nuria in her home, I am not likely to get a visa to visit Pakistan from the United States given the current political relationship between our two countries. That said, technology is a wonderful thing and we connect using FaceTime. It's 11 a.m. my time; 11 p.m. her time; our two lives are literally a world apart.

My very first question to her is about living as a woman in Pakistan and what might surprise others. "I think what people might be most surprised about is the number of incredible people in Pakistan -- as many dynamic women as there are in the west, you just have to know where to look.

Honestly, a lot of it has to do with social class and what people see in the media," she says. I ask her to elaborate. "Even with the young girl (Malala) recently getting a lot of press, shot for attempting to go to school -- that is most definitely an exceptional case -- it is not the norm by any means. However, a great deal of the disparity in young girls not getting educated is related to social class. In a lot of cases it is not something insidious (keeping girls out of school) it's more about financial restraints -- You keep the kids at home to help with the house work; it's more a result of conditions families are living in than not."

Nuria's seen first hand the importance of education. She trained professionally as an attorney and held positions with top international law firms and even a dot-com company, but took a break to have her first child. When her son was two years old, she went back to work, but in something completely different -- she became head of marketing for a NGO (Non-Governmental Organization) called CARE Foundation, an organization focused on educating the underprivileged children of Pakistan and running over 200 schools and educating over 150,000 underprivileged kids in Lahore. For over two years she ran their head office, and was in charge of raising funds, organizing events, dealing with donors and more.

"I really loved it," she says. "It was wonderful to be giving back. Often when I was doing my lawyering, although I really loved it I used to think that 'okay, this is fulfilling me mentally, but emotionally not really.' When I worked with CARE I felt so honored to have had the education that I had, truly valued the experience I had. I felt that in Pakistan I could really contribute." She stops for a minute and adds, "actually that is not fair -- you can contribute in the west too. I suppose what I meant was that I really felt that my contribution would make a difference. That is something special

about the third world; if you make the effort, you can see amazing results in such a quick time, and I think that is what keeps you going and does not allow you to get disheartened by the conditions around you."

Nuria continued working with CARE Foundation until her second baby came along. "I thought I would go back to work, but physically and mentally I could not. I am a hands-on parent and I love being there for my kids, so I took a break for a while," she says.

Then, everything began to change. Pakistan went through the rise of the Taliban and a place known for its peacefulness, the Swat District, was suddenly attacked by the Taliban and public beheadings and flogging of women started to happen and the government publicly passed a law allowing the Taliban to practice their own laws in a particular region of the country. The Taliban did not stop there and started to move into other locations. Nuria knew it was time for action. "At that point, myself and two friends felt enough was enough and we wanted to make the state wake up and take some action.

"There was a letter, written by a Karachi lawyer, addressed to the Prime Minister, President and others, telling them to enforce the writ of the state against the Taliban and punish them for their wrongdoings. We came upon this letter on the internet and thought it would be a good tool to get people into action, so we came up with the idea that this letter should be signed by a cut off date by anyone who was Pakistani, regardless of where they were living, and that if we could get enough people to do it, we could get the media to take notice, and more importantly, for the state to see what the will of the people was. This letter went viral, and there was probably not a Pakistani alive (who had internet access) who did not see it and did not put it into action. My original email that went out came back to me from places like Australia, Uganda, America, Canada, Germany, you name it! It was an incredibly empowering feeling – made me believe that each one of us has the power to change things, and if we work together, we can change things for the better quickly," she said.

In Lahore, hundreds of people physically turned up to the General Post Office at 3pm on the designated day and had their letters signed and envelopes stamped - the media had already had been alerted, and they came out in droves to photograph and interview of everyone. Nuria and her friends had managed to get the attention they wanted and got people talking sense to each other. Later, they organized a Prayer for Pakistan, with thousands of participants nationwide, including those in camps set up for those who had fled Swat District during the army operations there.

But Nuria and her friends were not done yet. They began emergency relief aid work, and soon realized they should give a name to what had now become a true organization. In April 2009, Pakistan Rising was born. "The next step was obvious," she said. "After we had supplied aid, the people we helped asked us to return to their villages, all of which were remote, and help them by setting up schools. We did the only thing you could do when someone asks for help -- we helped!"

Today, Pakistan Rising operates five primary schools for underprivileged children in Swat District and one in Uch Sharif in Southern Punjab, serving 700 children total. "I get really happy when I see the kids and I see they are learning and we are making a real difference. You see that education is the key," Nuria adds. Recently, Nuria organized and curated an auction at Bonhams auctioneers in London featuring 10 of Pakistan's leading contemporary artists which raised over GBP 40,000 for the schools.

Still she wanted more. "I wanted to help women -- given that I am a woman, and that I too understand what it is like to not be able to work because you are managing your home, your children, your family responsibilities, etc. I felt for the poor women in Pakistan who are mainly at home, who are not educated, and for whom it is very difficult to go out there and earn an income." To help these women, Nuria created a new venture, called "Labour & Love," combining business with a love for humanity. She works with impoverished women in Pakistan, training them and using their handicraft skills in a contemporary way.

Labour & Love creates a range of beautiful hand embellished items including sequined greeting cards, cushion covers, money envelopes, baby favor pouches, purses, shoe bags, advent calendars and t-shirts. Women are trained and are given all the materials they need so they can work from their home. They are paid per piece at a rate that is well above market. The organization gives the women the work, collects and checks the work, then pays the women immediately. "The idea is to make a profit but not such a great one that the worker is harmed in the process," Nuria says. "It always upsets me that so many women work from home, but often do not get a penny for their work, or are paid such a nominal amount, not at all fair after the hard work that goes into what they do." She's slowly building the business and loves the creativity involved. "Most of all I love the positive feedback I get from the women themselves – they love it, it allows them to contribute to their households which is a great feeling and they are active and doing something."

We talk more about being a woman in Muslim Pakistan. "The women here are so strong, so amazing...My mother in law went to Harvard Law at age 40. I find in my circle of friends that women's rights are always discussed. However, sometimes I get a bit irritated," Nuria continues. "As a woman, you get a lot of attention here whether you want it or not. The attention acts like an infringement on my freedom. Men stare so much that one does not feel comfortable going alone."

"However, in a strange way, men are very caring for women here. Yes, it's a bit chauvinistic, but I feel like a princess. If I go anywhere, they will clear the way for you. No one would dare allow a woman to carry a bag or a suitcase. In a very lovely way, you are protected. I know it sounds odd. Here in a country where it is perceived women are lesser citizens, you are given a special regard," she adds.

One of Nuria's main complaints is the misinformation that often goes with the Muslim faith. "Islam is actually an amazing faith for women. The biggest original converts were women; under Muslim law, they get the right to divorce and more. My faith is one that holds me in very high esteem. I don't feel like it's a faith that values me less than man -- quite far from it. It's just so hard when you have a population with high illiteracy -- they can't read the Koran for themselves. You are meant to read it yourself. The sad part is people don't read it and then listen to what someone else says to you...it gets misinterpreted all the time.

"We are a nation of over 180 million people. The actions of a few don't represent us all," she concludes.

- *Biggest Accomplishment*: My children for sure – one of the hardest and most difficult jobs, and of course the most rewarding, but I guess it is not really an accomplishment until they are all grown up and totally independent of me and are good human beings – then I will think that I have accomplished my job as a mother. Other than that, I think I have many things that I feel were great – the fundraising events and work I did for CARE Foundation, setting up Pakistan Rising and seeing the number of people we have helped through aid and Education; organizing the art auction at Bonhams for Pakistan Rising. But, maybe my biggest accomplishment is looking at myself and being happy with the person that I have become – which is actually a big deal when one sees that a lot of unhappiness comes from not being happy within.

- *Biggest Regret*: None – I don't believe in looking backwards. Everything, even those things which hurt us and cause us pain, play a part in how our lives unfold – it sure did in my case. Generally speaking I don't regret anything I did, since if those actions did not happen then I would not have experienced some of the amazing things that I have experienced. For example, with my career continually stopping and starting – sometimes I feel that I should never have stopped working in my legal career – I loved it, I was doing really well, I could have made a name for myself in it - but then I quickly backtrack and think no way, I would not have had those incredibly special times that I have had with my children which I would never swap for anything in this world, and if I had put my foot down and told my husband that no we would not move to Pakistan but would stay in Moscow and work, then Pakistan Rising and Labour & Love would never have happened.

⚊ *Biggest Surprise at 40*: Realizing that you have the power to do whatever you want – if you put your mind to it.

⚊ *What Would you Change if you Could?* I would change the way the world treats working women who stop their careers to have children – I would make it easy for them to be able to work part time. It is important that they get to experience motherhood and enjoy the wonderful things about it, as well as being able to work and get recognition for how brilliant they are themselves. I always think I should open a law firm which is only for mothers who are lawyers – everyone works part time -- you have enough people working on a deal so that the needs of the client are always met. Because at the end of the day, I think balance is what we all need – work and play, both in equal measure.

⚊ *What is Your Most Prized Possession (excluding family/children)?* It might sound corny, but my engagement ring. I used to joke with my husband, "bury me with it!" Now after having my daughter, I can give it to her. When I see it makes me remember the woman I became so that I could accept that marriage proposal, and also my life after I put on that ring - my marriage, moving country, my children, all these wonderful and exciting changes stemmed from that decision when we got engaged. It's something very special to me. It represents the path of my life.

What Would You Do With an Extra $100? Probably save it! **With an Extra $1,000?** Invest it in my business, Labour & Love. **An Extra $10,000?** Give some to my parents, and buy something lovely for my husband, myself and some other close relatives, like my sister and brother – then save some and spend the rest on a family holiday somewhere relaxing where sun and beach were on the agenda…as would be baby sitting and kids camps so I could also have a bit of a holiday too!

Penelope

Fort Collins, Colorado, USA

Sometimes I feel like I am still 18...Then I look down at my kids and wonder, 'How did this happen'?

Penelope always knew she wanted to be married and have two kids: A girl first, then a boy. Now, she's right where she wanted to be, mom to 6 ½ year old Ruby Skye and 20-month-old Linus. Married to her husband for more than 9 years, they both work at Fort Collins' New Belgium Brewing Company. Penelope's the more seasoned veteran of the pair with nearly 15 years of tenure at the brewery, a two-year advantage on her husband.

She's a "Mothership Hostess" at work, organizing and escorting VIP and private tours, mostly major distributors and even the occasional celebrity. She fits the bill perfectly with a sharp wit, engaging tone and genuine enthusiasm for the company she works for. Over her 15 years at New Belgium, she's had five different positions, starting in packaging on the bottling line, moving on to the fermentation cellar, then a brewer for a number of years, into recruiting in Human

Resources before moving into her new position three years ago.

You can tell the instant you meet Penelope she has the energy and zest most adults lose relatively quickly after entering "the real world." She credits her positive outlook on life to being "triple blessed – Living in a city I love, working at a place I truly enjoy and being surrounded by awesome neighbors in a community I am proud to call home."

On a typical summer evening when the Colorado sky stays dusky until well after 9 p.m., it isn't uncommon for Penelope to not even make in the front door when she gets home from work; she heads straight to the neighbors gathered outside with cold beer and snacks, watching the kids burn off their 'school's out' energy. Her neighborhood of 44 houses is home to some 40 kids and 25 dogs (give or take).

Being surrounded by her kids and all the neighborhood little ones gives Penelope a charge of energy – you can see it in her eyes when she talks about the camaraderie in her community. In a split second though, she'll look down at the kids running through her house, and suddenly wonder 'how did I get here?'

"I'm excited about turning 40 and feel more comfortable in my own skin than I ever have and feel like I really *know* myself, better than I ever have. Physically, I feel great...Sometimes I almost feel like I am still 18 years old, until a call from one of the kids or a quick glance in the mirror brings me back to reality."

Her and her husband's employment at New Belgium has positioned them well for the future. As employee owners, they are part of one of the dominant players in the microbrew industry. By the time she turns 50, Penelope plans to be looking at early retirement and getting a lot more traveling under her belt.

She's ventured to Belgium, Mexico and Belize, but has many more stops on her list, including Greece, Asia, Iceland and other parts of Europe. One of her co-workers has inspired her to get involved in her "15 year plan" that includes opening an artist-in-residence B&B/communal living property in Spain or France, the idea for which spun out of her co-worker's own trip to France and Belgium. "The idea of planning for something 10 or 15 years down the road is very appealing for me because we'd be heavy into it by the time I am 50 and my kids will be old enough then to travel to Europe with me. I want them to get out and see more since I didn't travel internationally when I was younger.

When asked about her life with the milestone number approaching, Penelope leans back and a warm smile spreads over her face. Looking off the balcony towards the mountains outside Fort Collins with a warm summer breeze on the air, she closes with: "I never thought it could be like this with my family, my community and my work; it's almost like a dream."

- *Biggest Accomplishment*: Meeting my soul mate (my husband) and having two beautiful, wonderful children. I feel fulfilled and blessed everyday for how my life has turned out.

- *Biggest Regret*: Never finishing college. I love the way my life turned out and who knows where I would have ended up if I did stay and complete my degree, but I want to make sure my children go to college and graduate. I also wish I had known my father better. He passed away when I was 23 and he was 81; he was 56 when he had me and we talked about him writing a memoir and we never did; those memories are gone now and I wish I had those details.

⅄ *Biggest Surprise at 40*: I never imagined I would work for a company for 15 years and never begin to see the end of it. When I moved out here at age 20 to go to Colorado State I really didn't know when I was getting into; I thought I would live here for a few years max, now no where else could possibly be home.

⅄ *What Would you Change if you Could?*   I wish I would have been active earlier in my life. In high school I was a string bean, into arts and music, not sports. My daughter's a lot like me. Now, I've gotten heavily into running and cycling and wish I had been active as a younger person so I could be fitter now.

⅄ *What Would You Do With an Extra $100?* I'm not good at saving, definitely somewhat of a wants machine. I would probably spend it on something for myself, most likely clothing or something for my bike. *With an Extra $1,000?* Probably spend a portion immediately on going out, put the rest aside to be a cushion as well as get something small for the kids. *An Extra $10,000?* I would pay down some debt, put some in savings, probably give everyone in the family the chance to buy something they've wanted for a long time.

Philippa, Nicola, Karen and Julie

The Women of Abu Dhabi, United Arab Emirates

A unique opportunity to sit down with four ex-pats living in the UAE all at once

Both Dubai and Abu Dhabi bring in scores of "ex-pats" – or ex-patriots – foreigners living and working in the UAE. Some come to teach, some for corporate positions, some to work in construction. It may be for a few months or a few years, but this large group of foreigners actually pushes Emiratis into the minority column in these major cities.

In Abu Dhabi I have a unique opportunity to sit down with four different ex-pat women, all relocated to the UAE after a husband's job opportunity or transfer. We meet one morning over the course of several hours at the stunning Fairmont Bab al Bahr hotel, perched on one side of the Abu Dhabi creek, affording a spectacular view of the Grand Mosque across the way. Philippa, Nicola, Karen and Julie each answer questions related to turning 40, as well as life in the UAE and integrating with local culture.

While each of their stories have unique elements, there are several common themes, including the surprise at ending up in the Middle East. "I had expected to be a wife

Philippa

and mother at 40, but certainly not living here in the Middle East," Philippa says. "We were living in London and because of economic conditions my husband took voluntary redundancy. He received a nice severance, so he was able to really take some time choosing a new position. The opportunity in Abu Dhabi came up and it seemed like an exciting chance to do something different and save some money --- there are no taxes here. There weren't a lot of jobs in London and so we decided to take a chance!" They originally planned to come three to five years; Philippa and her family have been here four years so far. "We really like it here, the job is going well and the lifestyle is fantastic," Philippa says. "It's much more sociable and we are able to go out more than we could in London because we are able to have help here – I don't know when we will go back," she adds.

Karen

The love of a more relaxed lifestyle seems to be a common theme amongst all the women. Karen's husband came for a construction job a few months ago and she took a break from a long-term teaching career to join him. She also echoes the relaxed lifestyle in the UAE but also appreciates the fact that she's not working currently:

"I'm wondering if I find life better because I have time. I always worked when my children were tiny. Now, I think, 'hey, I have more time,' and can do things I want both with my children and for myself," she says. "Earlier, I feel like we were on a much tighter schedule, with kids committed to after-school activities until 6 pm because I was working – now, I can pick them up from school in the early afternoon and do whatever we want, it's great!"

Julie agrees, and adds: "I definitely appreciate the lifestyle here because I was always working – I don't feel like I need to be working here. I think when people come out here, they have more time than they ever did and perhaps think they should be working. I have had people ask...'don't you miss it?' – no, not really! I appreciate spending time with the kids and having my own time," she says with a bright smile. She seems relaxed and breezy, this mother of three clearly enjoying the UAE experience.

While she's enjoying the time not working, Karen chimes in that she definitely plans to return to teaching, whether it is here, their next assignment or back in the UK. "Teaching is something that is part of you, it's not a choice. Whenever I go anywhere, I still think about things I could work in a lesson plan. I have always taught, even when I was a teenager, I would spend afternoons in school. I don't think I'll ever stop teaching," she adds.

Nicola is the most surprised of the group to end up living in Abu Dhabi. "I was a homebird, never living more than five miles from my parents my whole life!" she begins. "It all began a few years ago...We had our children and my husband has qualified as a teacher. We were sick of the weather in the UK, always cold and rainy, so we looked into getting a work visa to go to Australia. We had to move fast, because the cutoff is age 35 for the program we would qualify for. By the time we had applied, Australia no longer needed teachers and we were stuck," Nicola says. "I always said I would never live anywhere but Australia, even though I had never even been there – I was a typical Brit, wanted to live somewhere where they spoke English."

It appeared the family's plans were in jeopardy. "I didn't want to be anywhere else, but it became obvious the visa wouldn't come. We wanted an all-year climate. We started to think about Spain, realizing that learning Spanish would be a challenge, but then we found out that Europe's economic climate was the same as the UK's." The dream started floating away.

"My husband started looking for opportunities in other countries outside of Europe. "In my ignorance I was apprehensive about moving to a Muslim country as I worried the lifestyle may be too drastic a change from that to what I was used to in the UK". A job came up in Abu Dhabi. I remember thinking I had a friend who moved there from the UK and she helped endorse it. My husband accepted the job, without ever even going there!" she adds with a laugh. He planned a visit and took pictures and videos, and came home so positive about everything, it seemed like a good fit.

Nicola

The family moved a few months later and they are about halfway in to a three-year contract. "At the beginning, we said we would take it day by day, then week by week, then month by month...Now, we'll think about the big picture when the contract is up, but for now we are loving the lifestyle here!"

It's obvious that an attractive financial situation is a draw for most all ex-pats; jobs tend to pay very well, there are no income taxes and the cost of living is relatively low, allowing most families to pay for live-in help or child care. "As for many people coming over here, a huge incentive for us is definitely the financial rewards of living in a tax free country. There are many different things about living here as opposed to the UK but it's such a lovely way of life," Nicola adds.

It appears that all the women enjoy a much more relaxed, comfortable way of life in Abu Dhabi than they ever did in the UK, even if it means being unable to walk around as much due to the hot weather and less pedestrian friendly access ways (as Philippa added) or the driving – "lunatic!" as Karen calls it.

Julie and I talk a bit about the separation between ex-pats and Emirati women in Abu Dhabi. "You have to look at it this way – they are a minority in their own country," she says. "The curiosity about

Julie

foreigners you might see otherwise is not there. I have travelled to Oman and felt that the women were a bit more keen to engage there - perhaps because foreigners are more of a novelty.

That said, you do come across some open and friendly people here in Abu Dhabi," she adds.

It doesn't appear though that the separation is an intentional slight. "You might have an Emirati neighbor, but there are certain cultural restrictions between us that mean you simply wouldn't naturally mix. You don't realize how much of our social interactions have to do with alcohol or mixed company. There simply aren't so many natural opportunities to sit and chat. I have asked an Emirati friend about it and she says that some of it's confidence in English. We are chattering away in English, laughing and cackling. They might be quite good in English but they are hesitant to say hi. This is why learning Arabic, which many women do out here, can help break down some boundaries."

Karen interjects and asks the follow up question: "Do you think that is just more of a cultural difference between the UK and the UAE, where women might be raised to be less independent?" "Perhaps, but there are some very intelligent and articulate Emirati women out there," Julie comments. Even trying to meet other Emirati mothers at the childrens' school is a challenge. "Quite often its the maids that pick up the Emirati children, so we don't often even see them at school, where we might naturally mingle otherwise; many of the women are working," Karen says. "Even if you do see a woman in a social setting, it's hard to know what to talk about," she adds. "After a friendly hello, it's not like you can ask 'how's your hangover'?"

All four of the women have varying comments when it comes to turning 40 and what they thought their life might be like at this point. For Philippa, she feels the time has flown by since she met her husband in 2002 and got married in 2004. "My biggest surprise is how quickly the time has gone by since I met my husband; I have been very happy. When I divorced, I had a lot of fun but I think I wasn't truly happy. I was treading water. It was an exciting time but I missed having a soul mate. I always knew I wanted to get married and have children. I think happy time goes by quicker. The time here has whizzed past," she says.

Philippa also adds about the aging process for the body and turning 40. "I definitely notice a difference in my appearance; I work out a lot though to try to stay in shape. We spend a lot of time at the weekend by the pool or on the beach in swimwear so I like to be slim. When I look at photos from the past and I think that I complained how I looked, I realize now I looked all right!" she concludes with a twinkle in her eye.

Karen says she "never thought about turning 40" but that she still feels 18. She wishes she had explored more of the world when she was younger, but plans to be back in the UK at 50, probably retired.

Nicola laughs when she is asked about being 40. "I hate it!" she says jokingly. "In your 20s and 30s you have a perception of 40..it seems a lot older. It always sounded quite old. I didn't feel 40, whatever it's supposed to feel like. When I turned 40, I still felt in my 20s. In general, if someone asks my age, I don't like saying it! But, I guess now that I am here it is OK!" Physically, Nicola says she still feels as good physically as when she was in her 20s, but perhaps a bit more tired. She guesses it might have to do more with having kids than age. "When I worked full time in my 20s, then came home in the evening, I would say 'I'm so tired' – Now, I look back and think Jesus, it was so easy actually!"

Julie says she has "mixed feelings" about turning 40. "I can't believe that youth is behind me," she comments. I'm wistful when I think back to the craziness, fun, energy and strength of emotion I had when I was in my 20s and I know that is all behind me. It feels strange and a bit depressing to be looking ahead at 'old age.' That said, I am glad to be settled and to have finished with nappies and broken nights of sleep. I feel very secure in myself in a way I wasn't when I was younger. I'm proud of my family, friends and my career and I am still young enough and fit enough to make the most of life!"

What is Your Most Prized Possession (excluding family/children)?

⅄ **Philippa:** My photographs of my children...Because I have a terrible memory! (laughs) It brings back memories.

⅄ **Nicola:** I always think photographs – specifically of my grandparents that are no longer alive. You can always get more things but you can't get photos. I have necklace my mother in law gave me on my wedding day. She had a charm made of my beloved greyhound dog into a charm. It's very unique. It's something I wouldn't be able to get back. When we came abroad, we had so few things, four suitcases only. My most important photos I kept on me in case they got lost in transit. That way if everything else got lost those would be safe.

⅄ **Karen:** I have a letter, from a parent who when I first started teaching her child, really had it in for me; we did not get along. At the end of the year, I got a letter from the parent apologizing for her behavior and saying that I was the best thing that ever happened to her child. It makes you realize why you do your job.

⅄ **Julie:** I really can't think of anything more than folders of photographs. I am not great at taking photos, my husband takes more than I do! Having photographs of your children, your parents, yourself, your grandparents, friends. The more that time goes, things change, and having all of those things together visually is incredibly valuable and enjoyable to look back on.

Rosa Elena

Esperanza de Azama, Ecuador
"Birthdays do not matter…they are not celebrated"

Rosa Elena's window on the world is barely a porthole. Married at age 15 and now mother to seven and grandmother to one, Rosa Elena lives in a small community of 2,500 people outside the market town of Otavalo in Ecuador's highlands.

Rolling green hills are punctuated with clusters of brick and cement homes and fields of corn. This area is home to many of Ecuador's native Kichwa (Indian) tribe, who first inhabited this area more than 2,000 years ago.

Our interview was conducted in Kichwa thanks to community leader Margot, who is fluent in English, Spanish and Kichwa. We met with Rosa Elena at her home with six of her children, her grandchild and sister-in-law who lives just next door.

Her entire universe is only about 100 square miles. She has never been beyond the village of Otavalo – "I travel there once a week on Wednesdays to visit the market." She works making handcrafted beaded bracelets that she sells to market vendors for resale; her profit is $1 for each six bracelets made, a standard workday output for her.

On a typical day she rises with the sun at 6 a.m. to prepare breakfast for the family. Her kitchen is a simple pot, a fire and a few implements in her "kitchen/dining room" – a single three-walled space attached to the bedroom where all 10 people sleep in one Queen bed. After breakfast she beads for a few hours, and then takes the family's sheep down to the river for water.

In the afternoon, she again prepares a meal for the entire family (lunch), and again beads until the sun sets around 6:45 p.m. (being near the Equator, her sunsets and sunrises rarely shift more than a few minutes either way). Around 8 p.m. the family heads to bed without a dinner; two meals a day is the norm. "With the money I make selling bracelets I buy material or onions or vegetables to cook," she says. Most of the family's meals are vegetables and grain, with meat once a week on Sundays.

Some of the questions asked of other *Finding Forty* participants were not especially relevant to Rosa Elena's life where every day is a battle to survive. We did ask if 40 is a milestone number or of any importance. She laughs when the question is translated and shakes her head…"No birthdays are celebrated, they do not matter," she says. Many in the community don't know how old they are and Rosa Elena had to check her identity card to verify her own age.

When asked about how she might spend an extra $100, she seemed puzzled and overwhelmed at the thought of having that much extra money. After consideration, she responded: "Medicine." One of her children was ill in bed when we visited and her sister-in-law had just been diagnosed with uterine cancer at age 42.

Her husband was out of the house when we met, and his contribution to the household was not discussed. In the village of Esperanza de Azama, there is a significant problem with husbands abusing their wives, both physically and sexually. As a result, many women turn to alcohol to numb the pain and alcoholism is a widespread issue here according to community coordinator Margot.

After visiting with Rosa Elena, we spoke more in depth with Margot about this community and how they are surviving. "Most of the children will live here their whole life and are proud of the land. We are trying to get as many as possible in school. One thing we are proud of is that we all live in peace: Kichwa, Blacks, Whites, etc. However, the problem is the children now don't want to speak Kichwa; they are ashamed. I am fearful that we are losing our identity and in a few years all the indigenous people like Rosa Elena will disappear," Margot says.

Margot's objective and personal mission is to show families that their children can have a better life if they go to school. "When I was a child I walked to school with no shoes and washed my clothes in river. My mother was also an alcoholic. Someone helped me go to school, so I wanted to start a program so the kids could go to school. More than 100 children go to school now," she adds. "This community is a project of women -- A project for women to be leaders. Too often the men forget they have responsibilities and use their wives just as sexual objects." Unfortunately it appears a culture of cruelty to women is all too common and Margot recounted a story of a woman who tried to speak up and enjoy at least some sexual satisfaction. She was accused of being a prostitute and ended up hospitalized after a severe beating.

Looking forward, it appears a course of both standard and sexual education is the best way to help the women in this community. "All the women in my family got married at 14 or 15 and all my sisters are already grandmothers; one is only 34. We have to try to help so they don't keep having children." Regrettably, the men do not seem to agree. "One time I took 15 women to the hospital to get IUDs implanted," says Margot. "The men tried to hurt me, they did not understand. Thankfully my 20-year-old son defended me."

⅄ *Learn More*: www.caritasdeesperanza.org

Shamsa

Al Ain, United Arab Emirates
"I didn't think about what it meant to be turning 40, I left it for God"

Where to find a true Emirati woman? The quest had actually begun earlier in this trip, inquiring with all my interviewees in Dubai and Abu Dhabi about local women; it appears there is a real separation between the ex-pat and local communities and very limited connections there.

The road to finding Shamsa was a bit like a wander through the Arabian desert. I arrived in Al Ain full of hope, a traditional garden city nearly equidistant from Dubai and Abu Dhabi, on the Eastern edge of the United Arab Emirates and hugging the Omani border.

I begin by visiting the Al Ain Women's Technical College to attempt to speak with a faculty or staff member. While the young woman assisting me in reception was very kind, she informs me there are two women that are potential choices, but alas, both are on maternity leave.

Next, working with the George, the gracious director of sales at the Ayla Hotel, I am led over to the Al Ain branch of the Abu Dhabi Tourism Authority. After a few curious looks in the lobby, another lovely young woman listens carefully to my story of writing a book about women turning 40 around the world. Unfortunately, all the ladies in that particular office are years away from hitting the big 4-0.

The woman in reception does direct me over to the Al Ain National Museum, where there is a larger tourism office "full of Emirati women." After making the journey across town, I end up speaking with the front office staff at the museum and it appears that all the local Emirati women that used to work there have now moved on to a newly created historical village, about 10 miles out of town. Adding to the challenge is the fact that I will need a translator since I speak absolutely no Arabic outside of 'thank you'!

Drat.

The front office receptionist does ask me to hold on for a minute, because there may be a woman working at the museum that can help me arrange a translator. I thank them for their help and follow another staff member back through the facility and into the office where Shamsa sits.

The associate who brought me back to meet her says something briefly to Shamsa in Arabic then departs. I begin explaining what my book is about and how I thought she might be able to help me find someone to guide me in my quest to a local Emirati woman at 40 years old. She stops and ponders for a minute, then a small smile spreads over her face. "That is the age I exactly am!" she says. "You're kidding!" I exclaim. It turns out Shamsa just turned 40 three months ago and after a little begging, she agrees to speak with me. Incidentally, Shamsa in Arabic is "sun," and the warm glow of fortune was definitely shining on me to make this connection!

Born and raised in Al Ain, Shamsa's the youngest of five daughters. I ask her if she is married and she says, "no, not yet..." Then her male friend, who is joining us in the room to assist with translation issues, chimes in and says, "she's hoping, like any lady."

Shamsa came to the museum five years ago after the death of her father and currently works as an assistant store keeper with the Abu Dhabi Culture & Heritage Department. She studied social education at the university, graduating in 1998, but did not go to work right away. "I stayed in the home for many years," she said. "I took care of both my mother and father, who were older."

Over the course of nine years, she lost both her mother and father – mother to heart disease, father to Alzheimer's. "It was very sad to see my father like that," she adds. "He was almost like a child, needing so much help." First on Christmas Day in 2002, then again in 2007, she held each parent in her arms as they passed away. "I am not angry," she says. "God needed them."

A few months later she decided to go to work. She has enjoyed her work and also enjoys traveling extensively, especially for shopping. She's been all over the Middle East, as well as France, Switzerland, Italy, Austria, Thailand and more. "Milano...very nice for shopping!" she adds with a twinkle in her eye. Weekend excursions are also popular for her and her girlfriends to Bangkok. "We can get on a plane and in 6 hours we are in Bangkok, where the shopping is fantastic!" Shamsa estimates she's been there about 15 times.

She really would like to visit the United States, especially to see a niece who is being treated in the hospital in Washington DC, but the process for a visa is slow and it is nearly impossible to even get an appointment to apply for a US visa.

I ask her if she ever feels self-conscious wearing her traditional Abaya outside of the Middle East. "Everywhere there are good people and bad people," she says. "This is just what I look like, what I wear. I have been many places where no one even looks at me different. I did have one bad experience in Switzerland where a man kept bothering me and would not leave me alone for wearing my Abaya. I know though that he was just a bad person."

Now at 40, she feels happy, with more responsibilities at home though as she is the primary caretaker for herself, two sisters and one niece. She has a good income from her work, as well as being able to take her father's salary. "What I have I spread to all of my family," she says.

Shamsa did mark the occasion with a fun party and she comments it was quite fun, especially for a certain reason. I pause, look at her smile, and ask her if she is comfortable talking about what the special reason is. "Not right now," she adds with a laugh. We move on. When asked about life at 50, she says she expects to be back home again, no longer working.

As I am interviewing her during her work day, I try to be careful to not suck up too much of her time, yet I'm eager to get to know her better. We thank her translator friend, who leaves and we continue to talk.

"I love pictures," she says – and you can tell. Her office walls are filled with numerous photos of friends and family. "Pictures, pictures everywhere, she adds – On my desk, on my computer, even on my mobiles!" Shamsa has two mobile phones and we sit together and she shares her personal photos that capture her everyday life: Family gatherings, trying on outfits for weddings and special occasions, video snippets of children playing, favorite foods, funny street signs. It could be a set of photos right out of my own phone.

Through this gallery, I am able to see Shamsa's private life, including the fantastically glamorous clothing, makeup and jewelry often worn under an Abaya. Slides flash by one after the other – a gorgeous deep blue evening dress, a rich turquoise colored ball gown with equally stunning necklace worn to a friend's wedding, dramatically made-up eyes with impossibly long lashes, sparkling sets of diamond and gold jewelry so bright they almost blind even from her Blackberry!

I beg her once again to let me snap her photo as we chat, but she's having none of it. "No way!" she says emphatically. "Today I look very tired, I am fasting and have no makeup on...I will send you one, a proper one."

For far longer than I ever hoped, we sat together, sharing photos and laughing. Shamsa opens up to me, confesses she's a bit of an animal hoarder with 66 cats, 25 dogs, a monkey, turtle and a rabbit and even shared details about some very exciting changes to come for her this year, which I promised not to divulge! She does allow me to snap one photo of the two of us together on my cell phone which I keep as a souvenir to remember how similar we all are.

- ⚔ *Biggest Regret*: I don't have any.

- ⚔ *Biggest Surprise at 40*: That my mother died. It was sad, it was Christmas Day.

- ⚔ *What Would you Change if you Could?*   Nothing.

- ⚔ *What is Your Most Prized Possession (excluding family/children)?* My box of photos. It contains photos of my whole family, I like to look at it and remember people that have gone away.

Shannon

Jackson, Wyoming, USA
"Women are an absolute blast to take care of"

"You never know what is going to happen out here...This morning I admitted one of my patients, 33 weeks pregnant, to the hospital after an auto accident and her airbag deployed...A deer jumped out in front of her car on the way to work and she hit it head on!" As an OB/GYN in Jackson, Wyoming, Shannon has done it all, including following a patient to the hospital in a blinding snowstorm in case her labor progressed too quickly.

Shannon ended up in Jackson after finishing her undergraduate degree at Cal Poly San Luis Obispo in central California. She knew she wanted to attend medical school, but "felt like she should learn to live in the snow first." She decided to relocate to Jackson for a year before continuing her education and fell in love, both with the region and her eventual husband.

She took a retail job at one of the stores in Jackson's quirky, western-themed downtown square. Little did she know, her boss was the woman who would end up becoming her mother-in-law. After working in the shop for a bit, her boss begged her to "get her son out of the house on Monday night so she didn't have to watch football." In exchange, the woman promised Shannon unlimited snowmobiling that winter, something she was keen to learn.

The date ended up working out better than either woman could have expected: The two became engaged a year later and were married four years after that. Shannon and her husband Gib did the long-distance thing twice; first after their engagement while Shannon attended medical school at Saba University School of Medicine and then for four years after they were married as Shannon completed her residency in New Orleans. Gib worked eight months of the year in Jackson as a wild game butcher and spent the other four months with Shannon in the deep south.

Due to Shannon's hectic residency and work schedule, they waited quite some time to have their children. After Shannon and her partner opened their own OB/GYN practice in 2007, this duo moved forward to become family of four. Her oldest son Renny is now two and baby Brendan is just six months old.

Still breastfeeding, Shannon's schedule is a bit hectic and always up in the air. She's usually up at least once between midnight and 6 a.m. to nurse Brendan then read a book with Renny. Breakfast is often a quick snack on the way to work before rounds at the local hospital and a day filled with patients in the office. Of course, this can all be thrown out the window when a patient goes into labor, as was the case on the day of our interview.

Patient Rachel (also 40 years old) has gone into labor with her son so Shannon is back and forth into the hospital all day, checking stats and managing medications with the nursing team, preparing for a delivery sometime later in the evening. Shannon estimates she's delivered around 2,000 babies so far, about 100-115 per year.

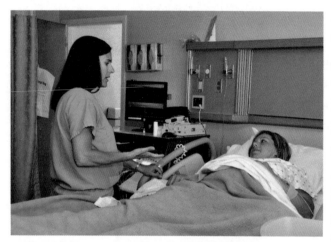

After medical school Shannon was originally going to pursue a residency in general surgery, but made the switch to obstetrics and gynecology because she found she loved the long-term relationships that came with this type of care. "Surgery is a blast, but after you remove someone's Gall Bladder, you never see them again. As an OB/GYN I get to become friends with my patients, seeing them multiple times during the pregnancy, delivering their babies, seeing them once a year and watching their families grow. It's awesome; women are fun to take care of."

Shannon says one of the reasons she loves working with women is feeding off the energy they transmit. "Women are the universal caregiver, the unit the entire family is built on. They have a unique level of compassion and I love working with them. As a mom, I think I can relate to my patients on a very personal level."

Although she's surrounded by women all day long, Shannon's psyched about raising her sons. "I am so looking forward to raising two boys and helping them grow into good, responsible men." She and her husband have no plans for more children – Gib is 47 and feels like two is a good number, although Shannon said she'd be game for one more, even past age 40. "People look at me with a bit of shock when I say I'd be open to another baby, but I think they're awesome and would be up to the challenge."

Truly, this mom-on-the-go seems to have boundless energy and doesn't have any plans for slowing down as the big 4-0 approaches. Moving through the hospital corridors she has a wave and smile for all her co-workers and stops to chat with several before popping into Rachel's room to see how her labor is progressing.

Beyond her everyday work at the hospital and her practice, Shannon spends three days a month visiting remote clinics in the rural communities of Pinedale (twice a month) and Thayne (once a month). Without hospitals of their own, women in these communities rely on Shannon's visits for routine examinations and pre-natal care. When the time comes for delivery, they will make their way into Jackson. At least once Shannon's had to meet an ambulance in route to determine if there was enough time to make it to the hospital. So far, she hasn't had to deliver any roadside babies, although she says "those are the easy ones...Mother Nature knows what to do and those just come on their own."

Shannon closes our interview once again apologizing for the scattered nature of her office before here eyes settle on one post-it note above her computer. "Half Naked and Pumping...Enter at Your Own Risk" it warns. "Geez, I'm glad you didn't get a close-up of that one," she laughs. "It warns the male medical students when my door is closed that if they come in they may find me in full pumping mode, bottling milk for my son...That's a day in the life right there," she concludes before scooting off to meet her first patient after lunch.

- ⚶ *Biggest Accomplishment*: My kids.

- ⚶ *Biggest Regret*: I wish I could have spent more time with each grandmother before they died.

⚮ *Biggest Surprise at 40*: How wonderful my children are. I marvel at how much I love them.

⚮ *What Would you Change if you Could?* I would be inherently more patient.

⚮ *What Would You Do With an Extra $100?* Donate it. *With an Extra $1,000?* Pay down some debt. *An Extra $10,000?* Pay down debt and put the rest to my sons' college funds.

Simona

Brescia, Italy

"No one ever asks a 40 year old man here why they don't have children or if they regret it. Why is it so with women?"

Where better to meet with a sommelier and wine tour leader than a cafe, in a lovely Italian piazza, enjoying a glass or two of the good stuff? We were fortunate to meet

with Simona just one day after her 40th birthday and we toasted her milestone and chatted about life in Northern Italy and working in one of the country's most important industries.

"I ended up a sommelier by chance actually...My school career was totally different!"

Born and raised in Brescia, Simona went to Trieste for university where she earned a degree in International Studies. "After school I actually was working in Environmental and Waste Management industries!" Her boyfriend at the time was studying to be a winemaker and was loving it. "He finished his studies and was offered an interesting job close to Naples. I wasn't in love with my current job so I decided to go too. However, once I got there I couldn't find anything I liked or fit my studies. The winery he was working at said 'why don't you work here?' – I didn't know anything about wine other than that I liked it!"

She started working at the winery and began taking classes to become a sommelier; the coursework takes three years total. "I started also working in public relations and with distributors and in the export markets. Many things changed in my life at that time." During her three years at the winery, she broke up with her boyfriend (they had been together 13 years, pretty much her entire adult life). "I realized we weren't meant to be but I also realized I really liked the wine industry." Simona began working for other Italian wineries but kept in touch with several people from her studies, including a woman named Genevieve who was there for an internship.

In 2003, she began working with Genevieve and her company, which was leading wine tours all over Europe – She came on board part-time to specialize in Italy tours. In 2007 she made it a full-time gig and now works exclusively leading groups and private tours through some of the region's most delicious tastes.

"Before I started this job, I had never been in the same position for more than three years. After a while I would get bored and needed to change the type of people I worked with, etc. Now, with this job, I am comfortable, happy and I can manage my time and that's the most important thing. I do something I like to." She credits her work as a tour leader in helping her grow personally and develop new skills. "Even if it's tough and it tests your limits, interacting with people enriches and can help in your personal life. I've learned to be more and more patient because of of this job. I am not a patient person at *all* and I have <u>learned</u> to be patient. In my personal life, I'm the sun; everything revolves around me. Now, I am not quite a moon, but at least more like an Earth!" she adds with a laugh that echoes off the cobblestone and makes me laugh just as hard.

One area where Simona knows she is definitely not ready for the patience required is motherhood. "I've been with my boyfriend for about eight years now and we are not married, and I don't want to get married. Definitely. Not ever. I know you are not supposed to say 'never say never,' but if I got married it would *really* surprise me. Luckily my boyfriend is OK with that." The two are not interested in children but she realizes that is more difficult to compromise about, especially in Italy. "That was one of the main reasons I broke up with my previous boyfriend. He wanted kids and I wasn't ready – I am still not ready! I guess I am one of those people who won't want something until I can't have it any more...So I am quite prepared that I will start wanting a child exactly when it is too late!"

The issue of not having children is a sensitive topic for Simona and amongst her friends. "I have some friends around my same age, some a little younger, some older, almost 50 years old. Everyone has a different idea about children. For some, you can't be a real woman if you don't have children. Personally, I totally disagree...I'm not saying they are wrong, that's just my own opinion. No one ever asks a 40 or 50 year old man here why they don't have children or if they regret it. Why is it so with women? You have intense social pressure if you don't have a child." According to Simona, the follow up she gets from people all the time is that she doesn't have children because her boyfriend doesn't want any. "You feel like they are saying it was someone else's choice you have to accept – you can really feel it here."

Simona says her mother knew she was never a little girl dreaming of the white dress and family. "She told me when I was like 5 or 6, I came right out and said that when I was 18, I would get my own apartment, and they could come visit but they had to make an appointment! I haven't really changed since then. When I was around 10 or 12, I started thinking about what it would be like to be a grown up, and it's really not so different than the life I have now – with a job, my own house and friends...An Italian Sex and the City!"

Simona does feel the pressure though of being a bit non-traditional. As if on cue, when we begin discussing the role of marriage and religion in the community, the church bells across the piazza begin to toll – we both laugh. "It's tradition to be married by 30 and have your children by 35. I may not be completely traditional but I am tied to many traditional things, like family." However, church is not part of her life. "It could be that I attended catholic middle school and high school, or it could be the fact that I don't like that someone else tells you how you are supposed to be." Fortunately for Simona, her family is supportive of her choices and they remain close.

"My brother is very close by – he's married, with kids. He works a lot in the summertime -- Sometimes his wife and kids go on vacation without him because he is working so much. He comes back to my mom for lunch and dinner every day and he's 45 years old – That's the kind of guy I could never be with!"

She's happy that her current boyfriend's values mesh well with her own at this point in her life. "It was quite difficult when I ended my 13-year relationship at 30 years old...It was all I had known. I didn't think about the future. I started to become more independent and appreciated new things. When I was 30 I was focused on the now, and maybe tomorrow, not 10 years ahead. That being said, I haven't really thought about being 50 either.

"In 10 years, I hope to continually appreciate life like I am doing now." Enjoying the last little bit of our drinks, I ask her which is her favorite wine – "Piedmont wine – a lot! There are lots of good wines no matter what kind. I really like Barbara – In a book, it was called 'The Worker Grape' and I really liked that description." I find I can't finish without asking one last question: Do you ever get sick of wine? "Yes – Totally!" she adds. "Sometimes after a tour, site inspection or wine fair I get a little bit sick of it...But that doesn't apply to food, for some reason. I try to detox myself but it doesn't last more than a week. If a friend sees me drinking something other than wine, they have to ask – What's wrong, are you sick or something???"

- *Biggest Accomplishment*: Probably that I am getting closer (still far) to a personal balance and that I still have many goals to accomplish. If I can accomplish a goal, I can have a further one to shoot for.

- *Biggest Regret*: I regret probably that I haven't fought enough for something I really care about; in some ways I feel like that could teach me something. Right now, I would like to be more patient and honest with myself.

- *Biggest Surprise at 40*: That you survive through everything.

- *What Would you Change if you Could?* On the purely superficial side: I have gained weight again after a successful diet. For a more in depth level, all the right things and all the mistakes I've made so far took me where I am, so I wouldn't change anything.

- *What Would You Do With an Extra $100?* A nice dinner out with a nice bottle of wine. *With an Extra $1,000?* Nice weekend somewhere. *An Extra $10,000?* A really great vacation.

Syd

Los Angeles, California, USA

"I never expected I would be doing this with my life and yet, it's amazing. I love it so much."

Syd's life now in Los Angeles is nothing like what she imagined it at 30 and she's happier than she ever thought she could be. "I'll be honest, the milestone of 40 has been freaking me out a little bit, but I feel now like everything fits," she says. In her late 30s she decided to change her path. Syd had been working almost exclusively in the entertainment industry as an independent filmmaker, gaffer and lighting designer. She liked the work but something just wasn't right.

"I decided to examine my life and find my space. At 35, I was in a session with my therapist and she asked me to vision my life at 40 and I told her she was crazy...40 was a long ways away," Syd says. She had ended a very serious relationship with her girlfriend and needed to figure out what made her happy. After a lot of soul searching she settled on a new career – one as an energy healer, life coach and intuitive reader. What does that mean?

"Basically I help people clear their space – whether it be mental, emotional or physical to help them make more centered choices for themselves." She's converted the second bedroom in her rented 1920's art deco house in Los Angeles into a healing space where she conducts individual sessions with clients.

Her downstairs living room also doubles as a meeting space where she leads group meditation nights. "I want to create safe places where people can try new things like meditation and creative seminars."

In addition to her independent client work, Syd is also adding regular hours at a metaphysical center in Los Angeles, working with an instructor that guided her through her own energy training. Independent films and creative work are still a regular part of her work and the occasional contract gig or film project fills her free time. "I just went out to Joshua Tree with my Super 8 camera to shoot an experimental film...it felt good to let my artist side be really excited!"

"This is where I was supposed to be...If only I had figured it out at 20!" Syd adds with an infectious laugh. "But I would not have had this wisdom at 20, I wouldn't be able to be the healer I am today. Spiritual energy is not something you just play with, and I use my life experiences, self knowledge and self love to help guide my clients."

Although Syd loves her new career as a healer and life coach, she realizes it comes with uncertainty. "I'm making it work," she says. Sometimes I am struggling financially, sometimes I feel comfortable...It always changes and the big picture is I am making it work." She grew up with a lot of privilege and has spent a chunk of her adult life choosing not to blindly accept it. Instead, Syd has worked as an activist for class equity and writes and blogs frequently about the inequality in today's society.

"I realized I am driven more by things other than money." She confesses she did however buy a Mega Millions lottery ticket when the jackpot swelled to a world record $640 million. "It was the first Lotto Ticket I had ever purchased!"

With or without a Lotto win, Syd is taking this time in her life to work on herself. "After my most recent relationship ended, I decided to take a break from all dating and really just focus on myself. What I want in a partner at this point in my life is so different than what I have ever wanted," Syd says. She doesn't have any children and doesn't want any. "I love being an auntie – it's the best." In a previous relationship she and her girlfriend talked seriously about adopting. "I'm glad I didn't do it...I wanted to have kids at one point but it was a different point in my life. I love my nieces and nephews but full-time parenting is not something I want to take on."

Syd is the oldest of five siblings from a very traditional Christian family and many aspects of her life have been met with resistance from her family, especially her parents. Coming out as as queer (how she identifies herself, as opposed to lesbian) in college, she started owning that term herself around 19, dating both men and women until her mid-20s, when she began seeing women exclusively. The journey was an emotional roller coaster, but she says through a lot of therapy and sitting with her siblings and parents things are much better now.

Feeling wiser and more confident in herself has definitely helped mend tensions with her family. "I am surrounded with friends I either grew up with or that have come into my life later on and many of us are turning 40 or have just made that leap and I realize we are all awesome! I find that the people I surround myself with now are doing what they want to be doing. The bigger picture for me is I know myself so much more now." She adds that with age comes relationships that just feel deeper and richer because everyone is bringing more of their essential selves to the table.

"When I was in my 20s, I thought life was complicated, but I would have figured it out by the time I was 40. I told my 50-year old boss this theory, and she said 'you'll never figure it out, you just keep working' – I was like, wow, that's disappointing. I was just thinking about this the other day and I actually think I was right...I may not have the answers but I finally feel like I have to tools to figure it all out," she adds. "I am now standing in my power."

After asking Syd about finding 50 a decade from now, she closes with a very empowered sentiment: "40 is kind of rad, but I think whatever coves next is going to be more rad – It's going to be exponentially better and more clear. I don't want to say I can't wait because I want to stay in the moment for the next 10 years. I see my work as a healer expanding, but I have no idea what I will look like. This joy I live with every day, even when things seem tough, is something that wasn't there before. It's joy from within, not something happening externally...it's great."

- *Biggest Accomplishment*: Learning to love myself and truly mean it. Truly, truly love myself.

- *Biggest Regret*: I keep my mouth shut too much. I spent so many years afraid of speaking my truth that I never did.

- *Biggest Surprise at 40*: That I am happy.

- *What Would you Change if you Could?* I wouldn't have been such a brat growing up and I would have learned Chinese. I wish I hadn't fought it so much as a kid. I would want to speak Mandarin and Taiwanese to be able to communicate with my grandmother.

What Would You Do With an Extra $100? I would pay bills. *With an Extra $1,000?* Portion would go to pay bills and regular debts. Maybe get my car fixed. I would give some away. *An Extra $10,000?* I'd take 25% for giving and use the rest for expenses and savings.

Traci

Chandler, Arizona, USA

"My kids and I have everything we NEED and MOST of everything we want...Which in my opinion, is a perfect recipe for happiness!"

Talk about just arriving at the 40 club -- we talked with Traci literally one day after she hit the big 4-0! Naturally, one of our main points is to talk about how she feels being 40. "It seems so surreal," she says. "I feel like a teenager most of the time, and my neighbor says I don't look a day over 32!" -- she adds with an emphatic 'ha!' -- "It just seems weird to think that I am "middle aged" now, but I think I better just accept it!

I just read something this morning that Elizabeth Gilbert, (author of *Eat, Pray, Love*) wrote on Facebook. She had gone to see a play called "Grace" the night before and had an interesting conversation with New York's Riverside Reverend…he said, 'Human suffering is often caused by a feeling that we have missed our path -- that we were meant to be somewhere else by now, but that some great injustice or cosmic mistake has placed us, instead, right here, exactly where we DON'T WANT TO BE.

In such circumstances, we often become paralyzed by grief, or overcome by resentment, longing for that which has not come to pass in our lives.' Reverend Phelps said that true peace begins when we accept that the path where we are now standing is the only road there is, and the only road there ever was. It doesn't mean you have to stay there forever, but it means 'This is where you are right now.' It is not an act of passivity to make that acceptance, but the opposite—an act of honesty, and a commitment to living within the real. Only when we have dropped the imaginary and accepted the real can we begin our true journey -- shaping and healing our lives in a positive way. I was very moved by this. It reminded me of the Buddhist instructor Pema Chodron's simple and beautiful teaching: "Start Where You Are". Traci couldn't agree more.

Traci is very honest and open about her past two marriages and and living within the real now. Her first marriage was to a man she calls 'her best friend,' but there was no physical attraction on her part, and the union only lasted a few years. "Not wanting to be intimate with the person you are married to obviously creates a problem," she said.

The second time around, she swung almost the complete opposite direction. "We had this very white hot, passionate romance," she says of her second husband. However, the basics of meshing personal values were just not there. "He was terrible with money and responsibility. Growing up, I think he was a bit coddled -- his parents were always there to bail him out and he never had to struggle for anything," she says. Traci, on the other hand, was raised to be independent, had always supported herself and never relied on a man to make ends meet.

"I'm not claiming that I was the perfect wife. I just felt like I was pulling way more than my fair share of the weight of the family. He is an artist and didn't make a lot of money, which in and of itself is not a crime, but he was terrible at budgeting. He always spent more than he made, and I always had to be the one to make up the difference. That gets old very quickly. It's one thing if a couple takes turns supporting one another, but it's another thing entirely when it's always the same person needing the support. I would try to make finances easier for him, even creating spreadsheets with all our bills and due dates -- he seemed to think due dates were suggestions; I just don't operate that way," she said. "Our personalities were just so different. I believe you have to work hard to make things work and he felt like things just worked themselves out. I ended up running myself ragged."

This fundamental philosophical difference ended up driving the couple apart. While there was the passion and connection she craved from her first marriage, Traci couldn't stay with someone whose values didn't match her own. "Among a myriad of other differences, the biggest was our attitude toward money...It didn't seem like he ever worried about the future -- I like to say he thinks about five minutes in front of his nose, and that's if he is planning ahead!" she adds with a laugh. In the end, the couple split up but Traci doesn't regret the marriage; it produced two beautiful children, now aged seven and five.

"I was hoping that the weight of responsibility of a wife and kids would help change his perspective on such matters, but it didn't. I wouldn't change it though; if I had waited to find someone who I thought was perfect, I might have been 40 with no kids and I really wanted kids." Her ex-husband is heavily involved in her children's lives and they split child-care expenses evenly now.

Naturally, our conversation turns to the question of a possible third marriage. "That's a good one," Traci adds. "I have been seeing this man (off and on) since I got divorced -- He's a great guy, really awesome. He would like to get married but I am scared to death of the whole idea. I look around and all I see are mostly failures. Everyone gets divorced! I've already got two under my belt!

I have come to feel like marriage is an outdated concept. At one point in history it was a good idea to pool your resources to help a family succeed. However, that concept seems to be changing. Women are more financially independent these days. Sure it's nice to have someone to share the responsibilities of the household with, but if it comes at the price of your happiness and sanity, then it isn't worth it. The problem with me is that I have gotten so used to doing everything myself. I also feel like as soon as couples make things legal, that's when they start taking each other for granted. To me, getting married is almost like giving someone permission to start treating you badly," she adds.

Traci continues, "For better or for worse -- what does that mean? What if it becomes for worse or for worse? Legal contract or not, I am not going to stick around and be treated badly; I don't want to be taken for granted. I want my mate to realize that that I am perfectly capable of walking away if it comes to that. Your partner is not a possession that you can just mistreat if you're having a bad day. You have to treat each other as if you're always auditioning for the part. I'd like some help and a partner, but not if having a partner means taking on the lion's share of the work necessary to make it successful -- my plate is already full!"

Beyond being a mom to two young children, Traci's plate is also full with a full-time job in the Arizona Air National Guard. She's been a Guardswoman for over 20 years, first joining the Air National Guard in Chicago in 1992. She had been working as a travel agent and decided she needed a college education and the military was a great way to pay for it. She worked as a drill status guardswoman for 10 years, then everything changed after the terrorist attacks of 2001.

"I had used my G.I. Bill benefits to attend Northern Illinois University and eventually transferred to Arizona with my boyfriend, who eventually became my first husband. I got a job at Arizona State University and after exhausting all of my GI Bill benefits, and was able to use my full time employee benefits to finish my degree in Anthropology at ASU. After the attacks of September 11, there was a call for volunteers to go on Active Duty orders to backfill for the security personnel on our base who deployed overseas. I was part of a Security Augmentation Team, carrying around an M-16 and everything!" A short time later a full time position opened up on the base and Traci took it, becoming full time Active Duty Air National Guard.

"I really like my position in the Air National Guard -- I get all the benefits of being active duty without having to move or deploy that often, unlike traditional active duty," she said. Traci has had several overseas assignments, including 30 day deployments to Japan and Qatar. "The nice thing about the Air National Guard is that your deployments are much shorter -- It hurt terribly being away from my kids for 30 days; I couldn't imagine being away from my kids for six months or more!"

One benefit of deployment is increased financial compensation. Air National Guard members get combat pay and hazard pay on top of their regular paychecks when they are deployed, all without paying taxes. "You are so busy on deployment, 12 hour work days, six days a week, often stationed far away from anything else, there's really no time to spend any of your money," Traci adds. As a result, Traci has been able to provide a comfortable home for her children. "My kids and I have everything we NEED and MOST of everything we want...Which in my opinion, is a perfect recipe for happiness!" She also accomplished one of her major financial goals, paying off her credit card debt before she turned 40. "I paid it off one day before my 40th birthday, so I guess I'm an over-achiever," she adds with a laugh.

- *Biggest Accomplishment*: My children, without a doubt. They are the most difficult thing in my life, yet the most rewarding. I hope I don't screw them up!

- *Biggest Regret*: Not knowing how far I could go in life and aiming for something bigger 20 years ago. Also not having higher expectations in the department of love back when (supposedly) the world was my oyster… It is such a true statement that youth is wasted on the young!

- *Biggest Surprise at 40*: I can honestly say that very little surprises me. Maybe the fact that reality is so surprising to others and their unwillingness to accept it surprises me.

⚹ **What Would you Change if you Could?** My patience level.

⚹ **What is Your Most Prized Possession (excluding family/children)?** I think of objects I wouldn't sell for anything, also something you would pull from your house if it was on fire. All my photo albums and baby books. Also, every day I wear two rings: They were both given to me by my ex-husband. One has my son's birthstone and the other has my daughter's. He gave me the first one to represent my son when I was pregnant with him and the second one he made by hand -- it's a female version of the first one. I take them off every night and have two or three places where I put them; If I ever can't find them, I panic. They make me feel like I have my kids with me at all times and I feel naked without them!

⚹ **What Would You Do With an Extra $100?** As long as I didn't owe anything, I might go get a massage or pedicure, or both! On my birthday, I got a pedicure and paid to have my car washed and waxed -- I was indulging myself, since I usually wash my own car and do my own toes. **With an Extra $1,000?** I probably wouldn't do anything. I'm all about saving now. I might take my kids on vacation. **An Extra $10,000?** Same as above -- save the rest!

Interview with the Author

As told by Rachel Gershwin; photographed by Jeff Stokes
"You don't truly realize how good your life is until you see how bad it could be"

With just a few weeks left before she turns 41, the creator of *The Finding 40 Project* reflects on her own journey to the big 4-0, and lessons learned along the way.

It's hard to believe that this world traveler, who has visited 46 different countries and logged nearly half a million miles in flights, battles a fear of flying that at one point kept her grounded for three years. "I had a panic attack when I was 26 on a one-hour flight from San Diego to San Francisco. I was on a business trip and spent the flight on the floor in the lavatory. I thought it was stress. That previous summer I had a few flights with rough landings, and before I realized what was happening, a phobia had developed. For my next business trip to San Francisco, I drove 9 hours each way for a two-hour meeting."

Three years later, after missing a good friend's wedding and passing up a trip to Hawaii to watch her sister run her first marathon, Aimee decided to do something about it. "I realized this was ridiculous, and that I had a long list of places I wanted to go, so I got help." She went through a 6-week flight therapy program, which was just the beginning of a long road back. "Phobias often manifest in type A women; oftentimes they are about a lack of control, which was my issue." Her graduation flight was a day trip with her mother to, of all places, San Francisco. By the Fall of 2001 she was "back in business" and planned a trip to Washington D.C. with her parents…fitting, as they're the ones responsible for planting her travel bug in the first place.

Aimee grew up primarily in Southern California. Her father was in the Air Force and the family loved to travel. "My dad keeps a spreadsheet of every flight each of us has ever taken, and he has personally flown over a million miles!" After graduating from high school in Huntington Beach, CA, she attended the University of Southern California, and followed a boyfriend to San Diego after college, where she began a career in PR. After a few years of working for firms, she realized that independence was a priority, started her own business and has never looked back.

Back to that trip to Washington D.C… They departed on September 8, 2001. On September 11th they woke up in their hotel room in Gettysburg, Pennsylvania and watched the second plane crash into the World Trade Center live on the news. "I remember yelling 'I wasn't afraid of terrorists until now, I was only afraid of flying!'" They drove their rental car across the country to get home. "After that I was more afraid of being alone than of flying."

Perhaps that fear of being alone is what led to the next chapter in Aimee's life, as it seems to be out of alignment with who she was up until that point. "I never thought my life would be traditional. I didn't dream of having a wedding and didn't think I would have children of my own, although I love kids and always imagined that children would be part of my life." But at age 30, Aimee got married. "I met someone and things moved quickly – we were engaged three months later." When asked why she married him, Aimee says,

"Because he asked...I thought that I might not have another chance and that I should get married." Less than two years later they were divorced. "That was a difficult time, but I learned a lot. I started figuring out what I really wanted in a relationship, and I learned to listen to my instincts."

After the divorce, Aimee started traveling more and took a one-month trip to Australia in 2006. "It was my longest flight ever and I traveled alone. When I landed in Sydney I cried, because I made it and I didn't let fear win." A growing love of photography was another catalyst to her international travels, which included a trip to Cambodia in 2008 that involved photographing the temples of Angkor Wat and local monks as part of a volunteer project.

"There is so much that I love about traveling. Meeting people, getting a peek into other people's lives, observing the daily life of other cultures and experiencing the traditions and foods of other countries. I love food, and it is such a big part of how we experience the world."

In 2008, Aimee met her boyfriend Jeff, a fellow traveler and avid scuba diver. "We met in October and took our first trip together in December - three weeks in Central America. People thought we were crazy, but it worked. We not only both love to travel, but we enjoy traveling in the same way." The twosome have since traveled around the world together, including a six-month sabbatical that took them to 18 different countries and included lots of scuba diving for both of them (Aimee took to the sport and is now a certified rescue diver). Other trips include Philippines, Micronesia and Palau in 2010, Honduras and South America in 2011, the Middle East in 2013, and many others.

In 2011, on a girlfriends' getaway trip to Sonoma in honor of a friend's 40th birthday, Aimee, who had just turned 39, started reflecting on the milestone and wondering what it might mean to women around the world. *The Finding 40 Project* was born. "The project combined my favorite things – traveling, photography and interacting with and learning about people." Her first interview was in May 2011 and although the mission has remained the same, the process has improved over time. "I wish I could go back and re-interview everyone from the first year, because I feel like I've gotten better at it since I began."

When asked what has been the most surprising part of the process, Aimee doesn't hesitate. "How open and honest women have been with me…opening their hearts and homes, sharing intimate details about their lives. This has been the most rewarding part of the project." And, although the subjects have come from vastly different circumstances, there are several common themes. "Universally, if women have a regret, it's around not completing something they were working on for themselves. Putting something else ahead of themselves. Women are far too often inclined to put themselves last, no matter what culture."

The project has also given Aimee a greater understanding of the role geography plays in one's destiny. "As a female, where you are born is probably the largest deciding factor in the destiny of your life. Being born in the U.S. is like winning the birth lottery…you don't truly realize how good your life is until you see how bad it could be!"

The project has certainly brought perspective to her own journey. "I've never been very worried about specific milestones associated with 40; I knew my life would be on its own path. Meeting women in other countries for whom 40 is just a number reinforced that in the U.S. we put a bubble around it. I met a woman in Ecuador who truly didn't know how old she was!"

Aimee describes 40 as better than she thought it could be. "When I was 30, I was married and thought I might have kids. I thought of life at 40 as somewhat more limited in scope. Now, at 40, I am nearly 40 pounds lighter than I was at 30. I feel better, look better, sleep better, am smarter and healthier. I thought I'd feel older." She looks towards 50 with positive anticipation and a goal of being as independent and free as possible. "People I know who are the most unhappy are the most dependent…on a job, on people, on things or other outside factors for happiness. For me, happiness is independence and a life that includes doing work I love, traveling to places I love and spending time with the people I love!"

Biggest Accomplishment: Physically, it was training for and completing my first marathon. I was inspired by my sister and saw how she was changed by the accomplishment. At that point in my life, I had only run 4 miles; I was not a runner and didn't know if I could do it. Mentally, my biggest accomplishment is getting over my fear of flying.

Biggest Regret: Not listening to my instincts more often at various times in my life.

Biggest Surprise at 40: That I am super happy in a long term committed relationship. Because I am so independent, I didn't think I was capable of spending so much time with another person.

Most Prized Possession: My passport! Every stamp represents another journey and another step away from fear.

What Would You Do With an Extra $100? I would go to my favorite taco shop, Lolita's, and treat everyone there to some food. **With an Extra $1,000?** Take my best girlfriends on a fantastic weekend getaway. **An Extra $10,000?** I would put it aside for my nieces, ages 7 and 11, to travel. I actually already have travel funds for them…I want them to experience new things and be exposed to life beyond California.

6302878R00081

Made in the USA
San Bernardino, CA
05 December 2013